CHASING THE HEAT
50 YEARS AND A MILLION MEALS

BY LEONARD GENTIEU

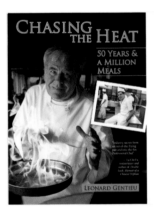

**Thank You
for purchasing CTH**

Please visit Amazon.com
and post a review

*Help me keep the
Journey going!*
~Chef Len

cookinone@gmail.com
Cell 805-441-1400

sandcat
publishing

Author's Note

Except when it's not, this memoir is intended to be a fun read. While it's based on actual events, some incidents and personalities have been embellished for dramatic effect, and some names have been changed to protect the innocent.

Leonard Gentieu
Morro Bay, California
_____ 2013

Email--- cookinone@gmail.com

Website--- morrobayboat.com

Chasing the Heat
50 Years and a Million Meals

©2014 Leonard Gentieu

ISBN-13: 978-1-63110-069-7
Library of Congress Control Number: 2014949445

Printed in the United States by
Mira Digital Publishing
Chesterfield, Missouri 63005

Praise for Chasing the Heat

"I have known many people I would call a good friend, but you can count on one hand the ones I call great, true friends. Len is one of my great, true friends. Knowing Len for all these years has been fun and an education. Because of him, I have never been able to walk into a restaurant and not think about what is going on in the kitchen. I am still like a small child listening to the Old Wise One telling his stories about his life and times as a chef. I love *Chasing the Heat* and it has been a real joy reading the drafts of his upcoming book about his life. Chef Len, thanks for being the great person you are and all of the great meals I have tasted that you have made."

— Ron Denner, owner of Denner Winery,
listed by *Wine Spectator* as the eleventh best
wine in the world (Jan 2012)

"Dining out? Here's a glimpse to the secret world of chaos simmering behind the swinging kitchen doors. Prepare to be astonished."

— Lynn Carter, retired president, Capital One Bank; board member,
American Express Centurion Bank.

.

"[Chef Len's abalone is] one of the best things I ever tasted."

— Dave Matthews of the Dave Matthews Band.

"Rare insights. Medium mellow dramas. Well done restaurant view. Seasoned with love and laughter. Served fresh."

— Bruce Schwartz, retired CEO,
Sysco Foods, Los Angles

"Industry secrets from an out-of-the-frying-pan and into-the-fire Professional Chef, including how to survive the undertow of the hazardous waters of the business. As Leonard comments in Chapter 6, 'I wasn't going to take anything for granted. The ocean can seem calm on the surface when there is a raging current just beneath.' Leonard charts the undertows encountered in his perilous journey, many of which are familiar to those of us who've survived (and at most times thrived) in the restaurant business."

— Lu Chi Fa, restauranteur and author of
Double Luck: Memoir of a Chinese Orphan

Table of Contents

Dedication vii

Acknowledgements ix

Foreword xi

Born to Cook – an Introduction 1

Chapter 1: Any Port in a Storm 3

    Sidebar: Food for the Gods – Dishes I Couldn't Live Without 7

Chapter 2: The Day from Hell Begins 9

Chapter 3: My Beginnings 13

    Recipe: New England Clam Chowder.................................... 18

Chapter 4: The Day From Hell – Revolt of the Tilt Skillet 21

    Sidebar: Throwing Away Money 23

Chapter 5: In the Country of Clubs.. 25

    Recipe: Southern Fried Chicken.. 28

Chapter 6: The Day From Hell – The Good News and
All the Other News 31

    Recipe: Grilled Hot Dogs... 36

Chapter 7: Cooking for the General 37

Chapter 8: The Day From Hell – Wet Pants and Other Distractions 43

    Sidebar: Tools of the Trade 46

Chapter 9: The First Deli... 47

Chapter 10: The Day From Hell – Not the Toilets! Yes, and More!........ 53

Chapter 11: Gentieu's Gigantic, Gastronomical Delight 57

    Recipe: Gentieu's Gusher 62

Chapter 12: The Day From Hell – Invalid Order! Manager Required! ... 63

    Sidebar: The Invisible Revolving Door.................................. 66

Chapter 13: Leonard in the Sky with Diamonds................69

    Recipe: Fried Rice à la Chu 73

Chapter 14: The Day From Hell – One Small Piece of Romaine............75

Chapter 15: The Show Must Go On 79

    Sidebar: The Money Matrix 81

Chapter 16: The Day From Hell – Floods, Flags, and Forks...................83

Chapter 17: Apocalypse Leonard's 87

    Recipe: Rack of Lamb with a Garlic/Tomato Reduction
    and Date-Fig Mint Jam 93

Chapter 18: The Day From Hell – War and Weeds, and Something
  Worse 95

    Recipe: Thanksgiving Turkey with One-Pot Mashed Potatoes 99

Chapter 19: Apocalypse Part II................103

    Recipe: Sauteéd Abalone 107

Chapter 20: The Day From Hell – What? No Fries? And Other
  Felonies................109

    Sidebar: Foxes and Wolves................113

    Recipe: Corned Beef, Cabbage and Veggies................114

Chapter 21: Mother's Day................117

    Recipe: Flaming Coffee à la Gentieu................122

Chapter 22: The Day From Hell – Free Wine and That Sucks 125

Chapter 23: In the Country of Clubs, Part II................129

    Recipe: Serrano's Chili Verde................132

Chapter 24: The Day From Hell Finally Ends 133

Epilogue................139

Afterword 145

VI

Dedication

To the millions of food service workers across the nation that prepare food and serve us every day. This book is dedicated to all of you. Thank you for your service.

Acknowledgements

I would like to express my thanks to the many people who helped me through the process of writing and publishing this book. My gratitude to those who provided support, brainstormed with me, read, wrote, offered comments, assisted in the editing, proofreading and layout of the text.

I would like to thank my wife, Midge, for her tireless efforts computerizing my hand-written draft. I want to thank Kitty Kladstrup and Hoyt Barber for walking down the gangway to the Papagallo almost three years ago and encouraging me to finish the book that I started 26 years ago. I deeply appreciate the support, guidance and encouragement from my brother, Larry Gentieu and sister, Ellen Dugan. Without their help along with several bottles of Three Sheets to the Wind, we may never have gotten to the finish line— I love you guys! I am grateful too for the outstanding editing work of Stan Pinkwas and Nils Parker. I'm very thankful for connecting with my "Dream Team" from Southern California, Leah Cooper of Armadillo Creative, Jennifer Silva Redmond and her husband Russ who were an absolute delight to work with; Jennifer doing her magic taking the book to final edit, Russ photographer extraordinaire and wine connoisseur and Leah's creative genius on design and layout. Thanks also to Catherine Meredith, John Konrad and Jeff Eckles for all their help through the proof reads. Special thanks to Sally and Mike Thompson for all their encouragement along this book-writing journey. To Lynn and John Carter for making their beautiful home in Cambria available for brainstorming on this project and others and for the fine wines brought from their cellar for our enjoyment. My thanks to Bruce Schwartz for providing the Foreword; Lu Chi Fa for the book cover quote; Lynn Carter and Ron Denner for their endorsements. Thanks to Jill Mettendorf, Senior Publishing Consultant at Mira Digital Publishing, for joining us in the production, printing and marketing phases. A very special thanks to all my past and present employees and co-workers through this 50 year plus journey in my food career. "Thanks for putting up with me during the good times and the bad." To my customers over the years at my many restaurants—thank you for your business. Last, but not least, I beg forgiveness of all those who have been with me through this adventure over the last couple of years and whose names I have failed to mention.

Foreword

There are people in this world who need no introduction. They come into—and enrich—your life completely by chance, a fortunate convergence of time and place, that would not have been the same had it been formally planned or arranged in advance. Such is the case with Leonard Gentieu. He needs no introduction because once you meet him, you feel as if you've known him all your life.

I first met Len in the 1970s when I was on my way to becoming CEO of Sysco Foods in Los Angeles. Len was running his first restaurant, Gentieu's Pantry, in Taft and I was a young, some would say know-it-all "food guy," intent on exceeding existing sales goals and becoming number one in the industry.

Although I had never met Len before then, you could say that we recognized each other almost instantly, as if reality had issued an inner mirror that allowed us to see more than just what was on the surface. What I saw in Len then and continue to see in him today is the real deal. With Len, what you see is what you get. Always.

Part of what I see is: His Integrity—Len's as good as his word. His Dependability—if Len says he'll be there, he'll show. His Honesty—there is never any question, whether it's the high quality of his food or the terms of your agreement. His Performance—Len's a professional who demands as much from himself as his employees. And last, but certainly not least, three traits that I believe are the key to his success and to the success of any entrepreneur—Enthusiasm, Passion and a Sense of Humor. Without these you're doomed to being number two. Len has them in spades.

In spite of a childhood that was less than ideal, Len has a great zest for living. He's good at it because he cares. About the people around him and about the task at hand, whatever it might be. It's done right. Or it's not done. He wouldn't have it any other way. Len gives as much attention to ensuring that guests on board the Pappagallo have music and a comfortable seat cushion as he does to making sure that the abalone is cooked to perfection. And this attention to detail is reflected in the book that you are about to read. He doesn't skimp on the truth or the humor.

(continued)

In *Chasing the Heat* you'll get a glimpse into Len's heart and soul as well as a real life, you-are-there-behind-the-kitchen door tour of what really goes on before your appetizer or entrée arrives. In addition to the chaotic world of running restaurants, he'll take you on a culinary and food industry journey that begins with an early interest in food service (although he didn't grow up in this world), and ends on board a 70 ft. yacht in Morro Bay (although he had no previous sailing experience).

This is indicative of the way Len approaches life. He's not afraid of it. He embraces it with both arms open wide. He's willing to work hard and meet each challenge head on. Like the successful entrepreneur that he is, Len seizes opportunity or he creates it, often holding on tight for the ups and downs of the ride.

From gaining early experience and training at a hamburger joint to graduating from the Culinary Institute of America, Len speaks from personal knowledge. His is wide and varied. In addition to extensive restaurant experiences, Len writes about how it feels to cook for a General in the U.S. Army, run a deli in California and prepare Country Club fare in Delaware, even getting yourself listed in the *Guinness Book of World Records* with a group of Taft College students. His sense of adventure and escapades on board the Pappagallo demonstrate a fearlessness few gourmet chefs can duplicate.

And like me, Len shares an incredible respect and admiration for food-service workers and restaurant workers everywhere. Partly because both of us know just how tough this industry can be and how underappreciated these folks are.

I won't kid you. It's hard work. Long hours. Low pay. There are days when you're almost too tired to take your shoes off when you get home. As Len recounts in his hilarious "Day from Hell," you're always being tested.

But you know what else? It's worth it. When you're constantly being tested, again and again, and you pass with flying colors—as Len does and relates in this book—well, there's nothing quite like it. So, sit back, relax and perhaps be thankful that you don't have to prepare dinner for 100 people.

— Bruce Schwartz
Retired CEO Sysco Foods, Los Angeles
(First single location to do over one billion dollars in sales)

Born to Cook—An Introduction

"I always dreamed, never gave up...
even when times got tough
That's when I'd push it a little bit more"

— from "Born to Run" by Lynyrd Skynyrd

I was born to cook. Even as a teenager I knew that, and more than fifty years and a million meals later I have the same love of cooking I had when I started. I've owned and operated half a dozen restaurants and worked in many more, in every capacity from dishwasher on up. I've catered thousands of parties, managed the kitchen for a military officers' mess, run a country club for the corporate elite, and even taught cooking classes.

Over those five decades I've certainly seen the highs of the business—Gentieu's West, my second restaurant, was so busy after it opened that we ran out of food and had to close temporarily to restock. I have also experienced the lows—two of my restaurants failed, I lost another in a messy divorce, and I have faced the specter of bankruptcy.

As a youngster, my future did not look promising. I struggled in school, especially in reading and spelling. I dreaded spelling bees, knowing I would be the first eliminated every time, missing even the simplest words. Years later, like many self-made men of my generation, I discovered I was dyslexic. In a way it was a blessing, a relief to learn that my problem with spelling was due to a reading disorder, not because I was stupid.

Despite the dyslexia I never lacked the motivation to succeed. I always wanted to excel, but in what?

In the eighth grade I was the only boy who joined my high school Chef's Club. In the eyes of my classmates that made me a sissy—boys were supposed to try out for the football team, not make cookies with the girls. My father strongly opposed my choice, urging me to follow in the footsteps of my older siblings and prepare for college. But that all changed one night, shortly before his death, while he was helping me with my algebra homework. He realized I just wasn't getting it. Seeing how miserable it was making me to struggle with something I was unable to master, he put his pencil down, looked at me and said, "If cooking's what you want, be the best cook you can."

That was it. I already knew cooking was what I wanted to do. But acceptance, finally, from my father? That made it real. He made it possible.

I began working in restaurants before graduating from high school and discovered I didn't just like cooking, I was good at it. I also discovered that in this line of work you could eat what you wanted when you wanted to, work with lots of pretty girls (all of the servers were girls then), and you got paid for doing it. To an adolescent, what could be better?

It was only much later that I realized my path through life was as much internal as external, and that the destination mattered less than the trip itself. "We are who we are from the cradle and we're stuck with it," Steven Pressfield writes in The War of Art. "Our job, in this lifetime, is not to shape ourselves into some ideal we imagine we ought to be but to find out who we already are and become it." I was born to be a cook and my life has been a journey to becoming one.

This is the story of that journey. Of my life in the kitchen and out in the dining room, of the highs and the lows of the restaurant business, of the spectacular—lighting myself on fire in front of the President of South Korea—and of the incredible feat—creating the world's longest sandwich.

A satisfying, well-rounded meal needs an appetizer to get the taste buds going, a main course with some side dishes, a great wine to complement it, and a dessert to top it all off. This book is no different. As my story unfolds, you'll find recipes for some of my favorite foods, useful tips for cooks and diners alike, and a surprise ending that recharged my batteries and renewed my career.

What keeps all of us going in this very tough business is love for what we do: making great food and creating great experiences for our guests, day after day, year after year, through good times and bad. As you'll see, this involves a lot more than knowing the difference between rare, medium, and well done.

CHAPTER 1

Any Port in a Storm

"Just sit right back and you'll hear a tale,
A tale of a fateful trip."

— "Gilligan's Island" Theme Song

Chairs, lamps, and tables sailed across the salon, along with the half-drunk, half-asleep bodies of twelve of my best friends. I was hunkered down, wrapped in a blanket, freezing my ass off when the Papagallo II lurched violently, jerking us to starboard and setting us on a northwesterly course. I ran to the helm to see if we'd hit something. The first thing I noticed was the helmsmen at the wheel. I'd never owned or operated a boat before, let alone a 72-foot yacht like this one, so at first I was shocked not to see the captain at the controls.

"Where the hell is Captain Darby?" I yelled.

"He went below deck a few hours ago to get some shuteye," one of the helmsmen informed me casually.

"What's going on?" I asked them. "What's happening? Did we hit something?"

"A large wave hit us abeam and the wheel slipped out of my hands," the helmsmen currently at the controls said finally. "Spun us off course a little."

That was an understatement—our new course would lead us back to San Francisco or, if the captain pulled the wheel a little more to the left, out to Hawaii, for which we had neither the fuel, the food, nor the experience.

"Where are we?"

"Due west of Monterey Bay," another helmsmen responded.

"Monterey? It's two in the morning!" I was flummoxed. I was as drunk and sleepy as my buddies below deck, but I could still do math. This boat had two 270 horsepower Detroit Diesel engines that could get it up to 15 knots; 10-12 knots in unfavorable conditions. Monterey was about 75 nautical miles from San Francisco. We'd been on the water for hours—we should have been well past Monterey by this point.

It turns out, with the Captain absent, our course had taken on a zigzag pattern similar to the type old war ships used to evade submarine attacks. Apparently it requires some skill to maintain a course heading and keep a yacht motoring in a straight line. And that skill was in short supply.

Hearing all the commotion, Capt. Darby scrambled up from below and rejoined us. He took charge, apologized for the delay, and soon had us back on a south-easterly course. This was certainly enough excitement for me. The adrenaline dump that follows being flung awake and thinking your new boat is about to sink into the frigid waters of the Pacific Ocean finally arrived. I stumbled back into the salon and basically passed out.

Twenty minutes later, Tim, one of my friends, shook me awake.

"We have a problem." Not again, I thought. "It's Mitch," he said.

Mitch was another of the dozen buddies I'd rounded up as my impromptu crew for our inaugural sail from San Francisco—where I'd just purchased the yacht—down to Morro Bay where the Papagallo II would be docked. Rubbing my eyes, I followed Tim down to the head. The scene was not a pretty one. Mitch was crumpled in a heap on the floor, unconscious. Immediately, I knew we had a serious situation. His face was white as a ghost except where it was bloody. The toilet water and the carpeted deck beneath his head were both a deep crimson color. Tim and I tried to revive him. He did not respond.

Captain Darby joined us in the guest quarters head.

"What the hell happened?" he blurted out as soon as he saw the scene.

We seemed to be saying that sort of thing quite a bit on this voyage. Mitch had been using the head when the boat yawed over a big wave. He lost his footing, fell, and hit his head on the edge of the sink, knocking himself out.

The Captain kneeled beside Mitch to check for a pulse. When he looked back up at me, his face said everything: he couldn't find a pulse. I couldn't believe this was happening. All I'd ever wanted since I was a young boy was to own a boat. Now, fifty-plus years later, I was living one of my dreams, and it was becoming a nightmare.

Captain Darby radioed the Coast Guard. They told us it was too foggy to send a helicopter, and we should head to the nearest port. They recommended giving Mitch smelling salts to try and bring him around. Bring him around? I thought, he doesn't have a pulse! What good are smelling salts to a guy whose heart isn't pumping blood?

Monterey was the closest port and Captain Darby quickly calculated the distance and course to get there. I wondered if we would get there in time. How long does someone in Mitch's condition have? How was I ever going to explain this to Mitch's wife?

There was a mad search throughout the vessel for a first aid kit. Usually the first aid stuff is kept in a very obvious, accessible place, but we didn't know any of that. It was the middle of the night and all we'd familiarized ourselves with since we shoved off from the dock was where to put the ice and beer. Finally, someone found a medical kit that had smelling salts. We ran to the head where Mitch was laid out, still unresponsive, and cracked the salts open. I held them under Mitch's nose and held my breath hoping desperately .

Slowly, Mitch responded. Thank God, I thought. How would I ever run a dinner cruise business out of a boat that one of my best friends died in? I couldn't. We radioed the Coasties to tell them the news. They instructed us to ask Mitch a series of current event questions. If he answered correctly, they said, he would probably be okay. I forget what we asked him, but he aced it and we whooped with relief. We cleaned Mitch up, got some non-alcoholic fluids in him, and tucked him into bed in the Master Suite for the remainder of the trip. I couldn't help but sing the "Gilligan's Island" theme song to myself as we chugged toward home. We were minus the beautiful girls and had long passed the three-hour mark, but if this wasn't a "fateful trip" I don't know one.

The fog lifted at sunrise, just as we were passing San Simeon Cove, where I'd spent so many happy hours kayaking. Maybe I should go back to kayaking, I mused, and leave this yachting business to the pros. Maybe I should have listened to Midge. I shook off the doubts as quickly as they came. It was too late now. I was riding this wave for better or worse.

Just outside the mouth of Morro Bay Harbor, we hoisted several signal flags on top of the boat deck. After such a harrowing trip, I was not about to be denied a glorious arrival into port. All hands were on deck, even our wounded comrade Mitch. Captain Darby blew several blasts on the air horns, letting those on shore know we'd arrived. Unknown to me, our docking area at Virg's Landing was right in front of the grandstand for the Harbor Festival due to begin at 10 a.m. that very day.

The Captain motored up to the dock, hitting bow first. It was more like a controlled crash than a smooth landing, with us hitting the dock and the dock banging up against the pilings. The crew jumped onto the dock and scurried around as the boat bounced against the rough dock. Finally, they secured a spring line, tied up the remaining lines and, suddenly, we were home. Our 19-hour maiden voyage was over. We were safe, sound, and only a little beaten up.

Our loved ones shouted cheers and questions from the top of the gangway, after working their way through festival security. "How did it go, honey?" Midge asked, rewarding me with a kiss.

"Tell you later," I smiled, as the guys gathered their stuff to head home and get some much-needed rest. "I have a few things to finish on board here. Why don't I just meet you at the house?"

Back on board, I sat down on the aft deck, exhausted. The parking lot above the dock area was filling with hundreds of people. Music was blaring from the first of many bands that would entertain that day. I thought a little hair of the dog might do me some good so I poured myself a double. Sitting there, sipping my bourbon, I felt tired, discouraged, worried, and alone. This is a helluva way to start a business, I thought. What was I getting myself into? Should I just post a "For Sale" sign, and be done with it?

Finishing the drink, I locked up the yacht and was about to head home when the owner of the restaurant adjacent to the dock met me at the top of the gangway. His operation included Tiger's Folly II, the bay's only—and very successful—dinner cruise vessel. He had no idea who I was, but I knew him. I had done my homework and learned about the harbor's other businesses.

"That's a beautiful yacht," he said, greeting me. "Headed to San Diego? Mexico?" It was a logical question. Many of the yachts that stop in Morro Bay are on their way south for the winter season.

"No, this is my home port," I told him. "We'll be docked here. I'm opening a new dinner cruise and special events business right here on the bay." The news did not go over well. He ran through a whole litany of scare tactics: it would never work, someone else tried this a few years ago, everyone who's ever tried it has failed miserably.

"What makes you think you can do it?" he added. "You'd be better off making it a live aboard." When I didn't reply, his claws came out. "You won't last six months. You think you're going to put me out of business, think again. I've been here twenty-five years."

I bobbed my head slowly up and down, as if coming to agree with him. The guy was a half-foot taller than me, but he had picked the wrong time to do this. And the wrong man. This wasn't my first rodeo. I was—and still am—a well-seasoned restaurateur who is no stranger to the heat of the kitchen or business ownership. And standing there tired and cranky (and a little fired up from the bourbon), after 19 hours of fear and adrenaline, I was ready for action. I stopped nodding, and calmly replied.

"You know sir," I said firmly, looking straight at him. "I've been in the restaurant business over forty years and you will find me to be one tenacious son of a bitch! The only way you will see this fail is if they carry me down the gangway in a wooden box. I am all in, my friend, all in."

"Is that so?" he responded weakly.

"As far as putting you out of business, well, you are going to end up thanking me for the business I will send your way. My low end is far above your top end and the customers that can't afford our services will end up on your boat."

This stopped him and, after letting out a couple grunts, he walked away. We were like a couple of old dogs. He was defining the boundaries of his territory while I was trying to establish mine. I had plenty of fight left and, if the previous days' events were any indication, I was going to need plenty more. Before he got too far away, I shouted out to him.

"You know what I predict? You and I are going to become good friends." He shot me a skeptical look. "And to prove it I'm going to invite you on board to celebrate my six-month anniversary over a nice bottle of wine, my treat."

That exchange, with a stranger who was essentially my competition, on the heels of what was almost a complete disaster, was just what the doctor ordered. I felt better instantly. I knew everything was going to be okay. I knew because I'd felt this exact way before, twenty years earlier, at the end of what is still the single worst day I've ever had in the kitchen.

Food for the Gods— Dishes I Couldn't Live Without

"Since Eve ate apples, much depends on dinner."

— Lord Byron

Throughout this book are a few of my favorite dishes; many learned from other cooks, most I've served hundreds of times. For starters, two great shellfish delights, followed by an all-purpose snack, a quartet of full-bore traditional dinners, sides hearty enough to double as entrees, and a duo of decadent desserts. They've all earned their gold medals from years of real-world taste testing, and represent the professional pleasure I've experienced from making and serving delicious dishes to people who enjoy them.

What you won't find is a West Coast Larousse Gastronomique. My cooking style, like my recipes, has always been intuitive, taking measurements by eye, checking flavors and textures by taste, and knowing aromas by nose. In what follows, I offer each dish's basic ingredients, the techniques needed to put them together, and some useful tricks I've acquired over the years. I hope and expect readers will add their own touches to each dish as he or she prepares them.

CHAPTER 2

THE DAY FROM HELL BEGINS

"If you are going through hell, keep going."

—Winston Churchill

In towns and cities across America there are restaurants that have been family-owned and operated for generations. Some are so well known they've become landmarks, destinations to be visited by locals and tourists alike. The Tadich Grill in San Francisco. Rao's in New York City. Phillipe's in Los Angeles. The list is long. Their histories are as varied as the foods they offer, and each has stood the test of time. They stay true to their roots, serving only the finest cuisine, often cooked in accordance with closely guarded family recipes, and even in today's fast-food-dominated industry they stand out. My goal when I started in the business—my dream—was to own and operate a restaurant like that someday.

In 1986, Leonard's, my final restaurant, was enjoying its third consecutive year of success. Leonard's was a huge space, converted from an old sporting goods store in the small town of Taft, California. It required a bigger investment than any restaurant I had ever opened, but it was worth it because this was going to be my legacy. This was the restaurant that was going to stand the test of time.

The concept for Leonard's was fairly straightforward. I would incorporate the best offerings from my previous restaurant—Gentieu's West—with a high-end salad bar as the focal point of the main dining room. Salad bars were very popular at the time. Leonard's menu would offer items unavailable at other local restaurants: Alaskan King Crab legs, 20-ounce T-bone steaks, Fillet Oscar (steak topped with crab meat), blanched asparagus tips and Béarnaise sauce. On the dessert side, I created something called The President's Review—jumbo ice cream concoctions named after Lincoln, Grant, Jackson, and Jefferson. Leonard's would be the most modern, most elegant, best-equipped restaurant in town.

After eight months of expensive renovation, we opened in April 1983 to an enthusiastic horde of customers, well-wishers, and curiosity seekers. Opening week, Leonard's was packed, with a line of customers snaking out the door every night. It was the kind of experience every restaurateur hopes for and we loved every minute of it.

Less than a month later, we served our first Mother's Day Brunch. This gave my new wife Midge her first exposure to the busiest restaurant day of the year. We were mobbed, and any thought of keeping her chiffon dress spot-free went out the window after an hour or two in "the weeds" of service. Ultimately, May sales eclipsed $150,000, a great number for a new restaurant, especially in a small town. Buoyed by this success, it wasn't long before we went back to the management of the shopping center, to lease another 1,000 square-foot space next door to Leonard's. We knew exactly what we wanted to do. We cut an opening through the wall and, after a quick remodel, opened a new banquet space.

Business boomed, and it kept on booming.

Three years after that glorious bellwether month, I awoke with the first rays of sunlight and greeted the May day with a smile on my face and love in my heart. Leonard's was on its way and all my dreams—not just the restaurant—were on their way, too. My sweetheart Midge lay sleeping at my side, aglow in the reflected light from the gleaming brass headboard of our queen-sized bed. A fresh breeze blew through the open window, setting the curtains dancing.

As the clock ticked past 6 a.m., I kicked off the covers, ready to take on the day. I headed for an invigorating shower permeated by the refreshing scent of soap lather and shampoo. Even the shaving went well—no nicks, no scrapes, no razor burn. When the aftershave hit my face and I felt the rush of a cool breeze instead of the typical burning of lemon juice and hellfire, I knew things were going well.

My schedule that day was light. No large parties booked in the dining room; the kitchen was fully staffed and ready to handle the regular customers. If I had planned to spend all day in the kitchen I'd have picked jeans and a work shirt, but today I had a couple of appointments penciled in my calendar which meant it was time to be business-like—neatly pressed slacks, a white dress shirt with a tie, and my favorite Bally slip-on shoes.

Glancing at myself in the full-length mirror on the closet door, I saw a winner. Most days I wondered who was running the show, Leonard's the restaurant, or Leonard the chef? Today, there was no question. With a spring in my step, I was ready for whatever the day might bring. That's how I felt this morning, a morning as rare as a bottle of 1921 Chateau Pétrus. And anyone who has ever been near the restaurant business knows just how rare that is.

With a kiss from Midge, I was off. It was 6:40 a.m.

DAY
FROM
HELL

Buckling into my Pontiac Gran Prix, I adjusted the mirror, checked the gas and tuned in my favorite golden oldies station. The traffic was moving nicely, and I relaxed back into my leather seat. Usually I spent the half-hour commute planning the work day or devising menu ideas, but today I thought only of the pot of steaming hot coffee awaiting me at Leonard's.

At the first stoplight, I noticed the driver next to me looking my way. I greeted him with a polite smile and he shot back a sullen glance before turning his head to stare at the light. Who peed in his oatmeal?

That unfriendly glance was an omen of things to come. Before the light changed my windshield was hit by a massive bombardment of bird crap from above. These were not the dry sparrow-sized variety of bird droppings. These had some magnitude. Had I unknowingly ventured under a flock of migrating Canada geese? Had a California condor circled overhead, waiting for me to pull up to the light before unloading?

No problem, I thought. The Pontiac's powerful windshield wipers will have this cleaned up in no time. I flipped the switch. The long hard-plastic wipers jerked into action with a teeth-chattering screech that sounded like the condor who'd just taken a dump on my car being strangled to death. Clearly, the reservoir of cleaning fluid was empty. The thrashing blades were doing more harm than good, smearing the droppings into a blurry white mess.

The drivers behind me started leaning on their horns, meaning the light must have turned green, not that I could see it through a windshield caked with guano. As I sat there, stuck in the middle lane with my wipers flailing away on high, the beeping grew louder and longer.

Soon, I was able to move forward as the wipers cleared enough glass for me to see. The driver who had shot me the hostile glance was now grinning from ear to ear as he passed me. "Go to hell, pal." Little did I know I would be beating him there.

CHAPTER 3

My Beginnings

"A journey of a thousand miles begins with a single step"

— Chinese proverb

I was 14, still in high school, when I got my first job in the business. I went to work for the Federal Bake Shop in Wilmington, Delaware, the local branch of an East Coast chain of bake shops. It was a case of starting at the bottom and working my way up. And I mean that literally. It was my job to wash the baking equipment and refill the bake bins at the end of each shift. Each day that required going down in the basement where the supplies were stored and struggling up the steps to the kitchen, laden like a pack mule with a 50-pound sack of flour hoisted on my scrawny teenaged shoulders.

As I worked my way up the ladder of success in the restaurant business, I thought a lot about that first job. Why a bakery? Baking isn't really cooking. Cooking is an art, baking is more of a science. I don't remember why I took that job at Federal Bake Shop. Chances are they were the only place willing to hire me at the time. But as I started to put this book together, I discovered a much more interesting and elegant explanation: it was a family legacy.

My ancestors lived in the picturesque medieval town of Orthez in the Basque country in the foothills of the French Pyrénées. They were "chocolatiers," or chocolate makers, and as our family lore has it, one of their patrons was none other than Henry IV, King of France and Navarre, the first of the Bourbon line of French kings.

Henry's mother, the Queen of Navarre and Duchess of Vendôme, lived in Orthez. Befitting his status as a king, when Henry visited his mother he stayed in a castle, and as luck would have it, the castle was situated across the road from the Gentieus' chocolate shop, the *Magasin de Gentieu-Baillan.* One

day when he wasn't attending to affairs of state, Henry apparently stopped in for a bon bon, and as a result of this fortuitous visit, the Gentieus became chocolatiers to his court.

Today, Henry's castle lies in ruins, but his mother's sixteenth-century stone townhouse, the Maison Jeanne d'Albret, still stands, and is a local tourist stop.

Many years later, in 1860, Pierre Gentieu, my great-grandfather and 18 at the time, emigrated from Orthez to New York, and soon was fighting in the Civil War. After the long war he returned to New York, where he operated bakeries in Brooklyn and Manhattan before trying his hand at the restaurant business. In the 1870s, Pierre opened a restaurant on South Street in Manhattan. Because my great-grandfather's restaurant was sold in the 1870s and located on South Street, it is tempting to think that it later became the Paris Café, an historic restaurant with a colorful history still operating at 119 South Street near the Brooklyn Bridge in lower Manhattan.

According to its web site, Thomas Edison stayed there while he designed the Pearl Street power station, the world's first. When he was New York City's Commissioner of Police, Teddy Roosevelt was said to have stopped in from time to time. Other notable visitors included Annie Oakley, Buffalo Bill Cody and Butch Cassidy and the Sundance Kid. Not so notable visitors included the notorious Albert Anastasia and Louis Lepke, of Murder Inc., who, in the 1930s, like their modern counterparts, were reputed to have plotted their criminal activities over a good meal in a restaurant, presumably at a table facing the door.

In 1877, Henry du Pont, a fellow Civil War veteran and a grandson of the founder of the DuPont company, secured Pierre a job working in the company's powder mills along the banks of the Brandywine Creek in Wilmington. Coincidentally, Pierre and Henry had both fought in the Battle of Cedar Creek under General Sheridan. (Pierre was wounded in that battle, and Henry, a captain at the time and later a colonel, served with such distinction that he was awarded the Congressional Medal of Honor.)

After moving to Wilmington with his wife Binie and their four sons and two daughters, Pierre took up photography, and when not engaged in the making of black powder, photographed the DuPont powder yards and workers.

A century later the Hagley Museum and Library in Wilmington used Pierre's photographs as a guide in reconstructing the site of the original DuPont powder works, and many of his photographs are on display at the Museum. Pierre died in 1930 at the age of 88, having risked his life serving his adopted country during what is still its deadliest war.

Pierre had four sons, Frederic, George, Joseph and Francis ("Frank"), my grandfather, whose own son Frank was my father.

Unfortunately, my father's life was not as exemplary as Pierre's. Alcohol was his downfall, wine in particular, which the French are famous for both producing and drinking.

My father had his good points, always instilling in his children the values of honesty and hard work, but when he drank he became a completely different person, bitter and verbally abusive, who engaged in long tirades of shouting and cursing directed against the world and its perceived slights, which he all too often took out on his family, including me, the baby of the brood.

The youngest of seven children, I once asked my mother if my birth had been an accident. In her sweet way she told me I was a wonderful surprise, which I believe was intended to keep me from feeling unwanted. She never spoke ill of my father, and certainly honored her vow of "for better or worse." A kind and loving person, she was the glue that held our family together.

With seven children to support on an income that never exceeded $10,000 per year, my father supplemented his income by playing drums in bands in and around Wilmington.

Just as I would in the restaurant business, he had experienced highs and lows as a moonlighting musician. The high point came with an all-expenses paid cruise on the Îsle de France and a week in Paris with the Lou Caruso Orchestra, just before he got married. The low point was a stint in Wilmington's long-since defunct Tiger Cafe, where the piano was positioned about two feet in front of the rear wall of the bandstand to allow enough room for the band to duck behind it when the nightly fist fights broke out and the beer bottles started flying.

We had few amenities growing up, but my parents always managed to keep the seven of us children clothed, housed and fed. And early on we learned the value of hard work, which often took the form of budding entrepreneurship. The earliest recollection I have of getting paid for providing a service was the 2-cent deposit I received on the Coke bottles I returned when I went to the store to get my sister Ellen a soda and potato chips. In the summer, I picked raspberries and blackberries with my brothers and sisters in nearby Becker's woods and peddled them to the neighbors, a captive market, and in winter we shoveled snow.

Loading and unloading watermelons with my older brother Paul was the hardest work I remember growing up. Paul bought the melons at a wholesale produce market in Baltimore, and I rode along with him in his truck down the DuPont Highway and Route 40 to pick them up.

They were loaded in his truck by forming a human chain, each person in the chain tossing the melons to the next. The first man in the chain, who picked up the melons from a pile stacked on the ground or inside the tractor trailer they were shipped in, was black, and it was my first experience working with someone who wasn't white like me (later, in the restaurant business, it would be Latinos). The pace of the chain was limited by its weakest link—me. I couldn't have been more than 11 years old at the time, and it was all I could do to keep up while the pick-up man never missed a beat, tossing melon after interminable melon.

At a roadside fruit stand the melons were unloaded and stacked in piles shaped like pyramids on beds of crushed stone. To keep them from rolling, you chocked the bottom rows by kicking stones against each melon when you set it down. The pay for this back breaking work? A penny a melon. For loading and unloading an average load of five hundred you earned $5. While it doesn't sound like much today, it was a small fortune to an 11-year old kid.

After the ninth grade I went to learn food service at Brown Technical Vocational High School in Wilmington, Delaware.

While at Brown Tech I worked six nights a week at the Charcoal Pit. It was a grind that lasted three years, but provided income, excitement, a challenge, and praise. I was a quick study and a sponge for information, and with each increase in responsibility came an increase in pay.

But even though I was climbing the food service ladder, from dishwasher to fry cook, grill man, broiler man, cashier and finally to assistant manager, I suffered from feelings of inadequacy. No matter how well I did, I always felt I could have done better. I became a perfectionist, a trait fostered by my father in my childhood. It was pounded into all of us to aim high and strive to be the best. Good advice, but inadequately balanced by love and affection, it became a burden I carried into adulthood.

The Gentieus had a long history of working for the DuPont Company, starting with Pierre, who worked there for 36 years, until his retirement in 1912.

Three of Pierre's sons followed in his footsteps at DuPont—Frank, Joseph, and Fred, who became the superintendent of DuPont's Carney's Point plant in New Jersey, across the Delaware River from Wilmington. My father worked for DuPont as well, and drummed into his children at an early age the expectation that we, too, would work for DuPont.

After his death in 1963, it was my turn. In June 1968, following my graduation with honors from the Culinary Institute of America (the other CIA), I was hired by the DuPont Country Club to be groomed to fill the chef's position, the culmination of all I had worked for from the day I first toted sacks of flour at the Federal Bake Shop. For me, it was the pinnacle—becoming a chef was the most prestigious position you could aspire to in the food service business. Alas, I was drafted into the Army in November 1968 before I could realize this dream.

Even so, I gained valuable experience during my brief stay at the country club, and later put to good use the advice I received there from an experienced old-timer, who gave it in one word: "percentages."

16

THE CHARCOAL PIT, INC.
2600 CONCORD PIKE
WILMINGTON, DEL.

PAY STATEMENT

At the time this advice seemed puzzling, but its value became apparent when I opened my first restaurant. Any improvement in a restaurant's percentages—the cost of food, labor and overhead—even by only a small fraction, translates into a better bottom line. Knowing what your operating percentages should be, and keeping track of and controlling them, is the key to a restaurant's profitability. "Percentages" turned out to be one of the best pieces of advice I ever received, and I've heeded it throughout my years in the restaurant business.

When I started in the business it was nothing like it is today. There were no celebrity chefs on TV, no restaurant reality shows, and no upscale chains like the Olive Garden. Back then, working as a cook was considered a job for people with few other skills, with a pay check to match, so much so that cooks did not want to be seen in public wearing their whites, and changed clothes before leaving the restaurant.

None of that mattered to me. The harder I worked, the more it paid off. But there was a downside. There was no time for sports or school functions in my life growing up, not even the senior prom. I was always too busy working, and only attended my graduation from Brown Tech because my mother wanted to see me cross the stage.

The work ethic instilled in me by my father stood me in good stead. Working 17-hour days was not uncommon then. Year after year you cranked out the hours, perfecting your craft. Success was not always measured by your paycheck, either. Often, the compliments you received from diners, as well as the respect you earned from owners, managers and staff for a job well done, were the difference between a good day and a bad day. Beyond that too, loving the work was essential.

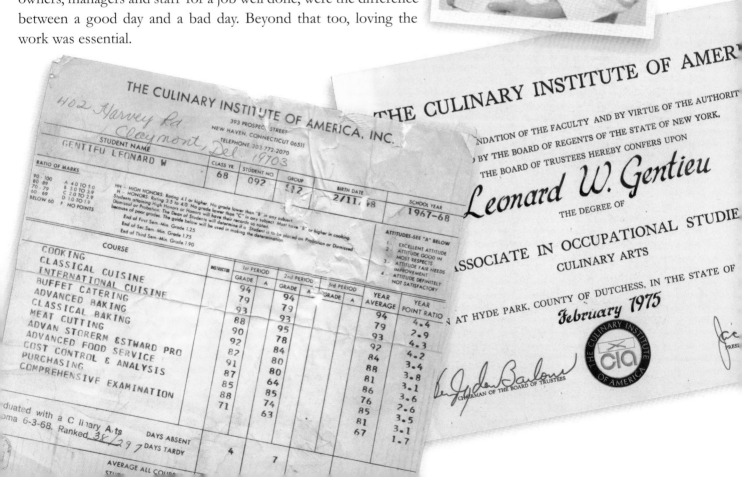

HOLLER LOUDER FOR YOUR CHOWDER

I worked as a second cook at the Carriage Drive Restaurant in Connecticut while I attended the Culinary Institute of America. One of my Carriage Drive duties was to prepare New England Clam Chowder daily for lunch and dinner. After making it every day for months on end, I got pretty good at it.

The fresh fish deliveries that arrived every morning always included one half or a full bushel basket of the quahog pronounced ("ko-hog") clams we used for the chowder. The label quahogs, scientific name mercenaria, comes from a Latin word meaning "wages," adopted because the Narragansett Indians, who originally inhabited the area, made beads they used as the money called wampum.

New England Clam Chowder (serves up to 10)

Ingredients

Fresh quahog clams (40 oz. if canned minced clams with juice)
2 cups clam juice
1½ cups celery
1½ cups onions
¼ stick butter
12 oz. bacon, diced
4 oz. salt pork, cubed (or 8 oz. Jimmy Dean hot sausage)
½ cup flour, approximately
1 cup milk
4 cups cream
4 cups raw potatoes, diced
1 tsp. ground sage
1 tbs. black pepper
½ bunch parsley, chopped
Oyster crackers (garnish)

Begin by washing the clams thoroughly, then place them in a stockpot one quarter full of water for steaming. When the clams open, remove the meat from the shells. Chop the clams, then strain them to rinse away the contents of the clams' stomachs and any residual sand. Strain the steaming liquid through cheesecloth and set it aside to add to the chowder.

New England Clam Chowder (cont.)

Today most restaurants skip this step, and instead purchase chopped clams that have been either canned or frozen, as well as canned clam juice or clam base. But nothing really replaces the flavor and texture of freshly chopped clams and the juice from their steaming.

Next, dice a cup and a half each of celery and onion and sauté them in butter until tender. Add diced bacon and a chunk of cubed salt pork or sausage; sauté an additional five minutes. Add flour to make a roux, the basic ingredients of which are butter and flour, to thicken and enrich the chowder. Keep the roux blonde by stirring while cooking it for about 5 minutes to remove the raw flavor from the flour.

With the roux cooked, add the warm clam juice to thin it, then milk and cream to create the actual chowder. When the chowder thickens, add diced raw potatoes and the chopped clams, simmering until tender. To finish, season to taste with small amounts of ground sage, black pepper and freshly chopped parsley.

If the chowder is too thick or too thin, adjust it by either adding more cream or more cooked roux. Serve the chowder piping hot, garnished with a small cube of butter, oyster crackers and a touch of fresh chopped parsley.

CHAPTER 4

THE DAY FROM HELL:
Revolt of the Tilt Skillet

"The real cycle you're working on is a cycle called yourself."

— Robert M. Pirsig

It was this love for my work—the restaurant, the people, the customers—that allowed me to brush off the sneering jerk along White Lane and completely forget about Operation Guano Drop by the time I pulled into my parking spot at Leonard's on that beautiful spring day back in 1986.

I noticed just a few unoccupied parking spaces—a welcome sign because a full lot attracts customers. With that many people at one restaurant, the theory goes, the food must be good. Every restaurant owner knows this and many drive through town checking their competitors' parking lots to see whose businesses are doing well. A friend who bought one of my restaurants took this a step further and paid someone to park across the street from my place and count the customers coming and going. He used this technique to estimate our sales, and I'll be dammed if he didn't nearly hit the number on the head.

Entering the kitchen, I extended my usual cheerful greeting to the breakfast cooks—an absolute must if you want to survive the ever-moody and temperamental cook who is responsible for not just keeping your diners satisfied but will be the one firing your order if you get hungry and decide you'd like a little something to eat. I've been on both sides of that encounter. It can get ugly, trust me.

Unfortunately, my handshakes and pats on the back were not met with smiles and hellos this morning. They were met with grunts. I had recently enrolled in a self-improvement course, and remembered the advice from the very first chapter: keep love in your heart for your employees, too, not just your customers.

Before I could pour a cup of the steaming coffee I had so eagerly anticipated, Margie, the first cook, informed me that the early day manager hadn't come in yet, the dish washing machine wasn't working, and the gas-fired tilt skillet wouldn't light, making it impossible to start the soup and lunch specials. Okay, this was starting to get ridiculous. First the jerk at the traffic light gives me the evil eye, then my windshield gets splattered with bird doo, and now all this. My wonderful day was starting to turn.

The tilt skillet obviously required immediate attention. Without even looking at it I suspected that Johnny, the night clean-up man, had accidentally put out the pilot light while he was cleaning the skillet.

The tilt skillet is a 30-gallon, square-shaped stainless steel cooking vessel that can be raised or lowered by a hand crank, making it easy to take out the cooked food. It's one of the really useful pieces of kitchen equipment, and most high volume, full-service restaurants have one. We added ours after our business grew.

The skillet can cook large amounts of food at a precise temperature, keeping the food from burning or drying out while it cooks. Ours was used for heating soups, sauces and stews, as well as batches of fried chicken, and for boiling potatoes for potato salad and steaming whole Maine lobsters, among many other indispensable uses. I don't know how we would have gotten along without it.

We also used it to cook beef tongues, the main ingredient in our pickled tongue appetizer. Pickled tongue was a regional favorite, and because of its popularity in the Basque community in nearby Bakersfield, we added it to our menu. The skillet could hold a full case of about two dozen tongues—after filling the skillet with water and immersing a case-sized batch in it, the tongues cooked at a slow simmer until tender. (As they heat up, the lickers rise to the top and poke out of the water—as if two dozen submerged bathers had suddenly decided to come up for air with their tongues sticking out—each many times the size of a human tongue.)

Ever playful, the cooks would spear one on a kitchen fork and chase the waitresses around the kitchen, wildly waving the huge, stiffened tongue at them. (Our cooks were also known to have engaged in this activity with live Maine lobsters.) The waitresses were good sports about it, laughing as they ran through the kitchen with a forked tongue in steamy pursuit, but looking back at these antics now, I'm sure some people would consider them disgusting, if not outright obscene. To us in 1986, such behavior, crude as it was, was just typical horseplay that went on in many a restaurant kitchen. Today, more likely than not, it would be considered sexual harassment.

The tilt skillet had to be up and running to prepare the day's soup and luncheon items, and since the cooks were busy preparing breakfast orders, the job of re-lighting the pilot fell to me. You would think that something like lighting a pilot light wouldn't be that difficult, but to light the tilt skillet's pilot you had to crawl under it. The last time its pilot light went out

THROWING AWAY MONEY

People are always telling me how great it must be to own a restaurant. I have a swell place to hang out, free meals, and I get to meet all kinds of people. Even better, I'm able to entertain friends and family while making lots of money. A subset of those people sell themselves on this image of restaurant ownership so much that it gets them just excited enough to open one of their own. Sure, they don't know the first thing about food, but there's always someone in the family who's a great cook or who makes the best apple pie, winning blue ribbons at the annual county fair. Their wife, mother, cousin, aunt or other inhabitant of the family tree invariably cooks up a storm at all their reunions.

Now, I love a home-cooked meal as much as the next guy. Most of it is comfort food, and memories of special dinners coupled with the instant recall of flavors embedded on childhood's taste buds cannot be duplicated at any restaurant. Consider, for example, my mother's turkey dinners at Thanksgiving. I've cooked thousands of turkey dinners over the years, but none like hers. After all, apart from taste, a multitude of influences conspire to keep home-cooked meals sacred—where you grew up, how the local foods were grown or raised, the water, the weather, various ethnic influences, and even the family itself.

In restaurant or club service, we create different memories than those made at home. If we're doing our jobs correctly, the meals we serve stay in people's minds as wonderful memories, but they are not home-cooked memories.

If you still think you want to open a restaurant (with or without Aunt Millie), my advice to anyone who hasn't already worked in the business for several years is to keep cooking—at home. If you don't know and love the food business and all it entails, including constantly ruining your good clothes, don't get into it.

Here's a thought exercise I use to explain the point more clearly. Faced with an eager wanna-be restaurateur, I tell them they can save tens of thousands of dollars on their start-up and continuing costs by first securing from their bank $5,000 in $100 denominations. That's 50 C-notes, a nice little fist full. Next, I offer to travel with them to a quiet street, preferably in the suburbs for privacy and to avoid the likelihood of being hit by a car. After locating a suitable manhole cover, I pull out a large iron bar, hook the bar in the slot of the round cover, and firmly push the bar down to leverage the cover up and away from the manhole.

Next, I tell them to start depositing the C-notes, one at a time, into the sewer. It's a thrill to watch the bills flutter downward and mingle with the foul-smelling sludge passing beneath. When their fist has been emptied, we're finished and the cover is placed back over the manhole. The whole thing takes about ten minutes. Heading home, we stop at a local watering hole for a drink, the perfect ending to this exhilarating restaurant adventure.

Think I'm just a curmudgeonly old dream stealer? Au contraire. I have shared this exercise with people who still went ahead with their plans to open a restaurant, only to return six months to a year later wishing they had taken my advice. Most admit that $5K tossed down a manhole would have been a much smaller loss than what they ended up losing. The failure rate on restaurant start-ups is over 90 percent, and my hat is off to the fewer than 10 percent who make it.

Obviously it can be done, hell, I did it. Multiple times. But not without a lot of sacrifice, hard work, psychic blood, and some real blood. A restaurant's a difficult and demanding mistress, and not for the faint of heart. Anyone wanting to start one and risk their money should think long and hard before taking the plunge. "I know of few businesses," says a restaurateur I know, "where you purchase perishable raw materials, house them, manufacture them, and retail them all in the same building."

DAY FROM HELL

there was a good deal of cursing before Albert, our dishwasher operator, managed to get it lit. Fearing a potential explosion if he attempted it again, I opted to light it this time.

After covering the floor with aprons I wriggled my way under the skillet and felt around for the red safety button that shuts off gas to the pilot when it goes out. When I found it I pressed the button, and with my other hand, pushed a rolled-up piece of burning paper through the pilot hole to begin the lighting process.

Once you light the pilot you have to hold the safety button down for about 45 seconds to heat up the thermocouple, and after that the pilot will stay lit and ignite the main burner. Only 45 seconds. That doesn't seem too long in the abstract, but when you apply it to constant physical activity, 45 seconds can feel like a lifetime. Try jump-roping for 45 seconds, or holding your breath. It's not easy at any age. It's even harder when your body's major muscle groups are twisted into something resembling a pretzel, like mine were underneath that damned tilt skillet.

I got the pilot light lit with the burning paper, but about 10 seconds into the countdown my finger slipped off the safety button, causing the pilot light to go out. Back to square one, I re-rolled and re-lit the paper, pushing it through the pilot hole to repeat the process.

Contorted and wedged into such a tight space, and depressing the safety button for all it was worth, I was suddenly hit with a tremendous leg cramp. This was not one of those slow rolling cramps that crawl up your leg. This was a white-hot dagger of torture. The kind of cramp that wakes you up in the middle of the night wondering why you are being punished. Part by part my body rebelled. My right leg broke ranks first and shot upward, causing my knee to hit the burner elements and knock loose thick black soot that hit me in the face. Forty-one, forty-two, forty-three seconds, almost there. My shoulder began to tremble. Only two more seconds and the pilot light would hold after I released the safety button. Forty-four, forty-five. With the countdown over, I took my finger off the button, and though I could barely see the tiny blue flame through soot-encrusted eyes, it continued to flicker gloriously. I slid out from under the skillet and cleaned up—but the tie had to go.

If someone I knew had told me right then, as I was dragging myself out from underneath the tilt skillet, that they were opening a restaurant I would have stared them right in the face and kicked them right in the ass—assuming of course my leg uncramped and cooperated.

CHAPTER 5

In the Country of Clubs

An' here I sit so patiently
Waiting to find out what price
You have to pay to get out of
Going through all these things twice

— Bob Dylan

In the late 1960s, with the Vietnam War near its peak, I received a student deferment to attend the Culinary Institute of America, shielding me from the draft for the two years I would be attending. Upon graduation, five job offers became available. The second best was as Chief Cook on an ocean-going tug working between New York and Florida. The position strongly appealed to my love of boats and the sea. But I had recently married and was about to start a family; the tug boat job would have kept me away from home weeks at a time. It was also likely Uncle Sam would come a-calling, as my student deferment had expired.

With all that in mind, I thought it best to be close to family. I accepted the position of First Cook at the DuPont Country Club, back in Wilmington, Delaware, where I'd grown up. If my father had still been living, he would have been pleased, but it was a difficult decision to return to my home state.

Over the course of my career, I've worked for two country clubs, one in Delaware at the start and the other in California after many years spent owning and managing restaurants. The first was as close to an idyll as I've experienced, the latter was among my toughest challenges. I learned from both clubs, but different lessons from each.

One lesson was that "the country of clubs" is not like the country in which most of the rest of us live. Unlike traditional restaurants, country clubs are private institutions whose members pay dues and fees. To some members, they're getaways, places to socialize. It's not unusual to see members spend entire days at their clubs, or show up several times a week for club activities. Business owners often use them as extensions of their businesses, with many a deal entered into between rounds of golf.

Country club staff usually know the members by name and address them personally and courteously. There's little room for error in pleasing the members, and staff need to be on their game 100 percent of the time. In return, cooking at a country club tends to be much less stressful than cooking on the line in a busy restaurant. In fact, working conditions, salaries, and benefits all tend to be better.

The DuPont Country Club was by far the classiest establishment I had worked in, up to that time. The kitchen was huge and filled with the best, latest equipment. The Club was the finest in the area and provided a great perk for DuPont employees. Club members could use the clubhouse and its restaurant, golf on any of three championship courses or swat tennis balls on a dozen-plus courts—and dues, subsidized by DuPont, were nominal.

The Grand Ballroom, where Sunday buffets were staged, was magnificent, dazzling guests with chandelier lighting reputed to have cost in excess of $1 million. The ballroom's hardwood flooring glowed with a mirror-finish gloss. A smaller Wedgewood dining room was available for group parties and Wednesday dinners. With light blue interiors, the Wedgewood Room was more elegant and intimate than the Ballroom. White plaster cameos adorned the walls and the window drapes ran from floor to ceiling. Everything was first class, from the furniture to the table settings, fine linen, china, glassware, and sterling table service.

The Club was open for lunch every day but Mondays, with dinners served only twice a week. Most work involved preparing the food for, and serving, banquets and golf tournaments. We also supplied food to a grill room on the lower level, where golfers congregated for lunches and snacks.

Henderson Ellis was the Chef. He was old school, an African-American cook who had come up through the ranks and paid his dues along the way. Even so, compared to most chefs at the time, he was mellow and wonderful to work with. One of his specialties was real turtle soup. (This was long before green turtles were an endangered species.) Whenever it was on the menu, Club members turned out in droves. Also on staff was Cornelius Taylor of New Orleans who taught me to prepare his special Cajun-style Southern Fried Chicken (find the recipe on page 28).

My first day on the job, Henderson instructed me to steam off three cases of eggs (45 dozen) for platters of deviled eggs needed for a large wedding party the next day. I was also assigned the task of making them. By the time I finished the nearly 1,100 deviled halves, I had become expert as the devil himself. By the time summer ended, I had become a valuable member of the kitchen.

The Club was closed on Mondays, and every Monday, during the single summer I was there, Chef Henderson and the cooks went fishing for sea trout in Chesapeake Bay. An ice chest full of beer, a pint of whiskey, and ham-and-swiss sandwiches on pumpernickel bread was standard fare for the trips. We would bob around for four or five hours out on the blue water, trying to hook the beautiful white-flesh trout called tide runners. The whiskey would be passed around with everyone swallowing a shot between beers. Henderson liked to lean over the side, coaxing the wary trout to strike his hook.

"Come on now fish, papa needs a nice pan-size for dinner," he would sing, almost like a chant. "Come on now, come on now, go ahead and take that hook. You come home to papa, papa needs to make mama happy." We ribbed Henderson, but he always caught the most fish.

That was the summer of 1968, the summer Robert F. Kennedy was shot; the summer police and anti-war demonstrators held pitched battles outside the Democratic National Convention in Chicago, as Mayor Richard Daly memorably declared, "The policeman is there to preserve disorder." That was the summer of the massacre at the Mexico City Olympics, the summer when students and trade unionists paralyzed France; the summer, even, of riots in Baltimore, only 75 miles from Wilmington. The summer before I was drafted.

Yet I remember the summer of 1968 as one of trout fishing in Chesapeake Bay, a summer of warm days, sun-washed, and magical. We all got along famously, insulated from the unrest taking place throughout the world. We were just a small group of cooks enjoying good times on our days off. What did we know?

My number came up in the Delaware draft lottery in October, and Uncle Sam beckoned. Soon, I was on a bus to Philadelphia for induction into the Army. The Country Club, which had been a joy to work for, assured me my position would be available at the completion of my military service. More than I knew at the time, my sojourn at the DuPont Country Club had kick-started my career, seasoning me just enough to be able to take advantage of the opportunity I stumbled into next.

Serving Suggestions

Traditional southern fried chicken is sometimes served without gravy and garnished with a mixture of minced garlic, chopped parsley and thinly sliced dill pickles. Another variant is Fried Chicken Maryland, which calls for a ladle of rich tomato sauce side by side with a béchamel sauce with the chicken pieces on top. Béchamel, one of cooking's mother sauces, is simply a blonde roux finished with cream and hot milk infused with the flavor of onion, bay leaf and cloves. Either way, fried chicken is best eaten immediately after frying to guarantee peak taste and a crisp texture.

TONGUE-SLAP YOUR BRAINS— SOUTHERN FRIED CHICKEN

I learned about southern fried chicken from Cornelius Taylor, a cook from New Orleans, when I worked at the DuPont Country Club during the summer of 1968. Chef Henderson Ellis always had Cornelius prepare fried chicken for the club's patio parties because it was so delicious it made your tongue slap your brains out, as they liked to say. Cornelius was gracious enough to share with me his recipe and method for Southern Fried Chicken. Now I'd like to share it with you.

Southern Fried Chicken

Ingredients:

3-lb. chicken, cut into pieces	Peanut oil
Buttermilk	Lard
Eggs	Chicken stock
Flour	Heavy cream
Salt	Potatoes
Pepper	Garlic, minced
Paprika	Parsley, chopped
Ground sage	Dill pickles, thinly sliced
Poultry seasoning	Tomato sauce
Ground thyme	

A three-pound cut-up chicken usually serves three to four people, depending on the number of pieces cut from the bird. If the chicken weighs less than three pounds, I always cut the bird into eight pieces, yielding two wings, two thighs, two breasts and two legs. Larger birds can be cut into 12 pieces by cutting each breast in half and each wing in half at the joint.

Begin by washing the chicken pieces in cold water and patting them dry with a kitchen towel. Place the chicken pieces in a large bowl, adding

Southern Fried Chicken (cont.)

enough buttermilk to coat them. I use two cups of buttermilk for one cut-up chicken, seasoned with a little salt and pepper. Add three eggs to the bowl to help bind the flour to the chicken pieces.

Take enough flour to toss the chicken pieces, and season the flour with salt, pepper, paprika, ground sage, poultry seasoning and a very little ground thyme. Taste the flour to adjust if necessary. Remove the raw chicken from the buttermilk mixture. Shake off the excess milk and place the pieces in the flour for coating. Remove the coated pieces and place them on a wax-paper lined pan ready for frying. Do not let them sit more than a few minutes.

For frying, use a black cast-iron skillet. This is one of the greatest, least appreciated kitchen tools ever developed. It's resilient, reliable and affordable, uses no moving parts, heats evenly and to a high temperature, works equally well on the stove or in the oven, cleans easily, requires little maintenance and if well cared for, will last forever.

Fill such a skillet half way up the sides with a mixture of about 80 percent peanut oil and 20 percent lard. Heat the mixture to 350 degrees. Using heavy-duty kitchen tongs, immerse the larger pieces first, carefully lowering one end in the oil and setting the other end down gently to avoid splashing the hot oil. Do not overcrowd the skillet. Almost submerge each piece, leaving enough room for the oil to surround it. Raise the temperature slightly if the oil cools too rapidly when the chicken goes in. Try to maintain the 350 degrees.

Next, listen closely. The frying chicken should crackle with an even, medium sound. Nor should the oil violently pop above the skillet and onto the stove. If it does, the oil is too hot and should be turned down. Some blood will ooze from the chicken, especially around the joints, during the frying. This is normal, and a good sign.

The chicken will usually be done within 20 to 30 minutes, depending on the thickness of the pieces and the temperature of the oil. Make sure the oil is not so hot that it browns the chicken too quickly, darkening the skin before it finishes cooking. To tell if a piece is done, pierce it with a fork; clear juice should rise to the surface. The best way to check is with a meat thermometer, which should reach a temperature of 160 to 165 degrees. Cooking the chicken past this temperature will dry it out.

If all the pieces won't fit in one skillet, it's best to fry in two or more skillets so as to complete the cooking all at once. When the frying is finished, transfer the chicken from the oil to a sheet pan and keep it warm

Southern Fried Chicken (cont.)

for service. If the oil will be used for another batch, strain it to remove the brown flour in the bottom of the skillet.

If it's not to be used again, pour off 90 percent of the oil, leaving the rest and the brown flour at the bottom of the skillet. Over a low fire, add some of the seasoned flour and stir with a French whisk to make a roux. Cook the roux until lightly brown, then add some heated chicken stock to make gravy, whisking to keep it smooth. Thin the gravy with heavy cream if needed. No other seasoning should be necessary. Serve the gravy ladled under the chicken, and over mashed potatoes (see Tradition Made Easy on page 98).

CHAPTER 6

THE DAY FROM HELL:
The Good News and All the Other News

It was evident that the dishwasher had a major problem. Bussed trays of soiled dishes were stacked everywhere. The servers, meanwhile, were shouting for clean silver and glassware. Albert was leaning against the machine, sipping a glass of not-from-concentrate orange juice—an infraction of restaurant policy, but his rap on the knuckles would have to wait till I found out what was wrong with the dishwasher. A quick assessment of a problem followed by corrective action is the hallmark of a good restaurant manager.

First, I had Albert set up a temporary wash and rinse station in the pot sinks to get the silver and glassware cleaned for the servers. As the sinks filled with water, I asked Albert what he thought the problem was with the dishwasher. The pump was in a bind, he conjectured, and not forcing the wash water into the spray jets.

Our dishwashing machine was a low-temperature model that sent two full racks of dishes or flat racks of glasses, soup bowls, or silverware caddies through three cycles, a pre-rinse, a wash, and a final rinse, where a no-spot drying agent was released. Because it was a low-temperature machine, the rinse cycle ran at 140 degrees Fahrenheit, hot enough with the added chemicals to sanitize the dishware.

Our machine was designed for dish washing only, but could accommodate smaller pots and pans. Machines designed to clean pots and pans are usually found in large hotels and bakeries, but even today, most restaurants wash their pots and pans by hand in scullery sinks.

Commercial dish washing machines are worth their weight in gold. Without them, everything would have to be washed by hand, increasing labor costs by untold hours and sharply reducing operating efficiency. So when a dishwasher goes down, it creates a huge problem with ripple effects that trigger even more problems.

DAY FROM HELL

Most managers and chefs know enough about dishwashers to troubleshoot common problems, and can usually get them up and running without the need for a service call. That's the best scenario, as it always takes the service guy more time than you have to show up.

A voice from the waitress station asked me if I would like a cup of coffee. "Make it black," I answered.

When I looked at the dishwasher it appeared that its pump wasn't turning, just as Albert suspected. Unlike the problem with my car's windshield washer, there was no scraping sound, and the dishwasher's tank held plenty of water. I pressed the reset button on the control panel to see if there might be an electrical problem. The shaft on the pump tried to turn, but jammed, telling me something was blocking the blades of the impeller, the rotor that maintained the water pressure.

I called the service man. He would be happy to help, there was only one problem—he was fifty miles away and working on a major repair at another restaurant. Since we needed the dishwasher back in operation immediately, I got down on the floor for the second time that morning and looked underneath the machine to see how much of a job it would be to drop the pump. Four large bolts held it fast.

"Albert, get me the crescent wrench from the storeroom," I asked my dishwasher operator. "The big one."

"It's not there," came his reply a moment later.

"That's the same wrench we use to change the CO2 tanks. Check the tanks in the main waitress station and see if it's there."

"Those night busboys never put anything back in its right place," Albert grumbled after fetching the wrench. Even kitchens have pecking orders and politics.

"Know what you mean," I agreed. Looks like we have more candidates for a knuckle rapping.

Sick of sliding around the kitchen floor, I perched myself atop an empty five-gallon pickle bucket and began loosening the bolts that held the pump motor. The first three came out easily. Piece of cake, I thought. Of course the last bolt wouldn't budge. I almost fell off the pickle bucket trying to break it loose. This single bolt was keeping me from seeing what was blocking the impeller blades, which was keeping the dishwasher from working, which was causing a shortage of clean dishware, which was creating slower service and unhappy customers. Our entire operation was grinding to a standstill thanks to one recalcitrant bolt.

My mechanical ability is nothing to brag about, which is one of the reasons I chose to become a cook, but I knew enough not to strip the edges of the bolt so much so that the wrench wouldn't grip it, and not to put so much torque into the effort as to break off the head of the bolt.

More tools would help, I thought. "Albert, get me the WD40 and a hammer," I asked him. When a man attempts to repair something he'll often resort to a hammer. I don't know why a tool designed to drive a nail provides such comfort just by having it at your side, but it does.

When Albert returned with the hammer and the WD 40 I sprayed the bolt, gripped it with the wrench, and was all set to start hammering away.

"Phone call for Len, is he back there?" Gloria, our assistant day manager, shouted from the front.

"Find out who it is and I'll call them back," I answered.

Gloria returned to tell me it was the newspaper rep, who wanted to know if our ad copy would be ready by today's 10 a. m. deadline. Debbie, our day manager, who hadn't made it in yet, was supposed to have taken care of it the day before. Just what I needed. I couldn't get machines or people to do their jobs.

"Tell 'em I'll call back in a few minutes," I said.

Focusing again on the hammer and wrench, I tried a couple of test blows before administering the wallop I hoped would free the bolt. My aim was off. The hammer grazed the end of the wrench handle, sending both wrench and hammer flying into a tray of soiled dishes and scattering broken glassware everywhere. Fortunately I missed both Albert and my thumb. When you work with your hands like we do, you can smash a pinky and go on with your day. Smash a thumb and it's game over.

Clearly another approach was needed. More leverage on the wrench handle. That should do the trick. Webster defines leverage as an "increased means of accomplishing some purpose," a definition that encompasses more than the mechanical action of a lever. Certainly it should apply here, I reasoned, as our purpose was clear, and the means of accomplishing it desperately needed increasing.

I remembered that we had a six-foot section of commercial PVC pipe in the storeroom. It had been left over from a remodel of the kitchen. It should provide more than enough leverage to break the bolt loose.

Albert fetched the pipe. Because of its length, we had to jockey it into position between the dishrack shelves and the stainless steel drainboards. That done, I clambered back on the pickle bucket, and after adjusting the wrench to fit the bolt head, slipped the pipe over the wrench handle, being careful not to disturb the fit of the bolt head in the jaws of the wrench. Albert had been holding the other end of the pipe, waiting for me to give him the signal.

Suddenly he cried out, "There's a spider crawling out of my end of the pipe!"

"Kill it!" I told him.

"With what?" he answered.

"Your hand! Now push on the pipe!" Albert pushed and the bolt broke loose, as did the pump's gasket seal. Seal broken, a shower of dishwater shot out like a soapy Old Faithful. I'd placed a container under the machine to catch the spill-off once I pried the bolt loose, but its placement was predicated on an orderly release of the bolt from its socket. I didn't account for the potential of a broken seal. The jet of dirty dishwater instead scored a direct hit on my dress slacks and Bally slip-ons, soaking them through before forming a surprisingly large puddle on the kitchen floor. A little more

DAY FROM HELL

than an hour into the morning and I'd already lost a tie, a pair of slacks and my favorite shoes. My banner day was quickly becoming a bummer day.

Still, I shrugged off the dirty deluge because, with the bolt loosened, I could finally see the pump impeller. Stuck in its blades were the remnants of a dish towel that had been sucked into the pump, the result of another infraction of restaurant policy—dish towels were never to be washed by putting them in the dishwasher racks.

I cleared the impeller, remounted the pump, and we were back in business. Even after demolishing a tray with the hammer, there were plenty of full trays of dishes left to wash, and Albert was thankful they wouldn't have to be washed by hand. As for me, there was a little less spring in my step and a little less starch in my collar.

And the day was just beginning. Leaving the kitchen, I grabbed another cup of black coffee and headed for the dining room. As I made my way to the waitress station I noticed that a good many tables were still filled. The early morning crowd was usually gone by now, and the next busy stretch typically didn't begin until 11 a. m. It looked like we were going to have a good day.

Then Gloria gave me the news that Debbie had called in sick. Now this created a big problem. Like the chef's, the manager's job entails a good deal of responsibility. We could adjust for planned time off, but with short, or no notice, it was much harder to get the shifts covered, especially when we were as busy as we were.

Everything seemed under control. Nonetheless, I wasn't going to take anything for granted. The ocean can seem calm on the surface when there is a raging current just beneath.

"Okay, what's not set up right now? Is there something I need to begin working on ?" I said to Gloria.

"Well I've got some good news and some bad news on that front," she answered. "Which do you want first?"

It's always been my experience that whenever I hear this expression the good news is never quite good enough and the bad news is awful. But I'm a positive guy. "What's the good news?" I asked Gloria.

"The Kiwanis Club just called in to reserve the Gaslight Room for a luncheon for 40 at 11:45," she answered. "They know it's short notice, but some regional muckity-muck is passing through town and they thought the luncheon would be a great way of getting everybody together to meet him. You need to call and go over the menu with them."

I was glad she booked the party. Hard as it would be to serve the party on such short notice, we never liked to turn business away, especially when the business was coming from the Kiwanis Club, many of whose members dined with us regularly.

"Here's the bad news," Gloria continued. "We have another party of 35 for a baby shower at the same time in the West Side Room, and Margie informed me the chicken breasts needed for that party were shorted on the morning delivery. We have no servers to work that party and we're already

short three on the main floor. One's out sick, one's on vacation and the last one has a scheduled day off."

"Have you tried calling someone in?"

"Yeah, but I couldn't get hold of anyone."

"Okay, just hold the breakfast servers over."

"I'm already doing that, and we're still short."

"Well keep calling. If need be, I'll help serve. And we can move a busboy off the floor to cover the baby shower. We'll make it work somehow."

Often we have to work through busy periods shorthanded. Managers must strike the right balance between having enough staff to handle the business and not being overstaffed, which results in a higher cost of labor. Most staff understand this, and will rise to the occasion to get the job done. In the case of the wait staff, a shortage of servers means added tips for those covering the shift, but those tips entail a lot of extra work, and are well earned.

"Len, there's more. I accidentally broke a key off in the change drawer in the cashier's stand trying to open it," said Gloria. "I was in a hurry to get a roll of quarters and put the wrong key in the slot. It got stuck, and when I wiggled it back and forth, it broke off."

"I'll look at it on the way back to the office," I said grimly. "For now, keep asking for change and tell all the waitresses to use their tips and keep track of how much they need to be reimbursed."

"Another thing," Gloria went on, "the night cleanup people forgot to sweep and mop the waitress station and we had ants this morning. I had Albert sweep and mop. That's what made him late getting the dishes started."

Good grief, will it never end?

"Anything else?"

"Two ladies in Booth 3 saw a cockroach scurry up the wall while they were having breakfast. They were so disgusted they couldn't finish their eggs Benedict and told Linda they'd never eat here again. Naturally they didn't leave a tip."

Fortunately the cockroach was on the wall and not hiding in the home fries, I thought.

"Remind me to call Orkin," I told Gloria. "I'll be in the office after I take a look at the change drawer. Buzz me on the intercom if you need me."

WHAT next?

THE GREAT AND LOWLY HOT DOG

Frankfurter, frank, wienie, wiener, red hot, Coney Island hot or dog. Call it what you will, I and virtually everyone else loves a good hot dog. Today, it's come to mean a cooked sausage usually made of beef and pork, though all-beef, turkey, chicken, kosher and vegetarian varieties are also available.

The hot dog's origin is cloudy at best. Some maintain the frankfurter was developed in Frankfurt, Germany in 1484. In 1987, Frankfurt celebrated the 500th birthday of the hot dog, which did not sit well with many in New Jersey, as the state has its own claim on the barkless dog. I leave who's right to the experts, along with the details of the sausage's ingredients and manufacture (often said to be best not known).

36

Grilled Hot Dogs

My favorite dogs are by Hebrew National, Farmer's and Oscar Meyer, all widely available commercial brands. If I'm in a hurry for them, I seldom eat just one. I'll boil a couple until they plump and while they're boiling, place a wire grate on top of the pot to steam the buns at the same time. In the summer I prepare the dogs by placing them on a cutting board, and rolling each one forward with a sharp knife, cutting through a quarter inch or so of the meat. This makes a spiral cut in the dog that, when broiled, causes the link to open up and evenly brown.

Grilled dogs are especially good overlaid with a piece of cheese at the last minute to create a cheese dog, although there's no end to the number of condiments and garnishes that can accompany hot dogs. I like them best with mustard and nothing else, my favorite being Moutarde de Meaux, a spicy whole grain version made by Pommery. My best advice: knock yourself out and get creative.

Accent on Dining Out

Chef prefers mustard dogs for at-home food

Friday, November 26, 1993

Accent on Dining Out is a weekly profile about Kern County residents and their interests in the arts, theater and music.

Leonard Gentieu owns Jaussaud's Catering by Leonard, a full-service catering business both at the restaurant, 1001 So. Union Ave., and at a location of the client's choice.

Q: What can always be found in your refrigerator?
A: You will always find hot dogs, orange juice and butter in my home refrigerator.

Q: When you're fixing yourself something at home, what do you make?
preparing potstickers,

CHAPTER 7

Cooking for the General

"Experience is the name men give to their mistakes."

— Oscar Wilde

Like my great-grandfather, I served in the military, but under vastly different circumstances. After basic training at Fort Bragg in North Carolina and a brief stay at Fort Ord in California, in 1969 I shipped out to Camp Red Cloud near the town of Uijongbu, about 13 miles north of Seoul, South Korea. Red Cloud was the headquarters base for I Corps, the Army corps charged with defending the western half of the Korean Demilitarized Zone (DMZ), the narrow strip of land about 160 miles long and 3 miles wide established as a buffer between North and South Korea as part of the armistice that ended the fighting on the Korean peninsula in 1953. Despite its name, the DMZ is the most heavily militarized border in the world.

I had been "in country" only three days when Colonel Arthur D. "Bull" Simons, a legendary Special Forces combat veteran, strode into the enlisted men's mess and out of the blue asked if anyone knew how to make Soufflé Potatoes.

"I do, sir," I piped up, not batting an eye at the question.

"Come with me," he said, "we're going to the general's mess."

One of the cardinal rules of being in the service is to never volunteer for anything, and that thought crossed my mind as I rode along with Colonel Simons in the jeep that took us to the general's mess. Who, in the middle of nowhere, would want Soufflé Potatoes? I wondered. And what if I screwed up trying to make them?

Soufflé Potatoes, or pommes soufflé, is a dish seldom seen in restaurants, and I had only made it once while studying to be a chef at the CIA. The finished product looks like two potato chips joined together with a space

in between. The trick in making them is to fry them twice, once at a low temperature and a second time at a much higher temperature. During the second frying, the potatoes quickly become crisp and form a waterproof skin, making the slices puff up as the moisture inside turns to steam. Their preparation has to be just right for them to turn out well.

When I walked into the General's kitchen, fried sliced potatoes were everywhere, flat as pancakes, none exhibiting the puffiness of Soufflé Potatoes. Having failed in their attempts to make them, the cooks were only too happy to let me give them a try, and my training came through; by the time I'd completed the last step, the potato slices were a golden brown and wonderfully puffed. After a light salting I placed them in a napkin "horn" for presentation, which was quickly whisked to the general's table.

He loved them, I was told afterward, and with this feather in my cap I was ordered to get my gear from the barracks and return to Headquarters Company. Just like that, I was made lead cook for the commanding general of I Corps, consisting of two American and three Korean divisions totaling 100,000 men armed with tactical nukes as well as conventional weapons. The commanding general, Lieutenant General William P. Yarborough, a West Pointer known as the father of the Green Berets, was a foodie before there were foodies and just happened to like Soufflé Potatoes. And as far as I knew, I just happened to be the only person on the Korean Peninsula who knew how to prepare them.

My most important responsibility was meeting with General Yarborough to develop menus for the official dinners welcoming visiting VIPs to the base. At the time, I only had a few months experience working as first cook at the DuPont Country Club, along with my CIA training, but quickly got up to speed by studying the gourmet cookbooks kept in the general's kitchen and the Larousse Gastronomique, an encyclopedia of mostly French cooking. This on-the-job training was supplemented by trips to Seoul's marketplace to buy fresh vegetables and other ingredients.

Shortly after I became lead cook, the mess sergeant was rotated back to the States. I was chosen to replace him and put in charge of eight enlisted men and 10 Korean nationals, and promoted to the rank of Specialist 5th Class. Unless awarded for heroic performance in battle, it normally takes much longer than the 14 months I had been in the Army to go from slick sleeve to Spec 5, but knowing how to prepare pommes soufflé got me there without a shot being fired.

In the general's mess I was responsible for the daily preparation of breakfast, lunch, and dinner for General Yarborough and his staff of thirty officers. He must have been pleased with the operation of the mess and quality of food served under my stewardship, for when he received orders for his next duty assignment, in Hawaii no less, he wanted to take me along as his personal cook.

It would have been a dream assignment, but to go with the general I would have to add another year to my term of service. I was a short timer, with less than a year to go, and couldn't wait to return to the land of the round doorknobs and the job I hoped would still be there for me at the DuPont Country Club. It was hard to turn down an offer from someone as distinguished as General Yarborough, but regretfully and respectfully, I did.

His replacement was Lieutenant General Patrick F. "Hopalong" Cassidy, who commanded "Cassidy's Battalion," an airborne battalion that distinguished itself in World War II, fighting at Normandy on D-Day.

Unlike General Yarborough, General Cassidy was strictly a meat-and-potatoes guy. After he assumed command, the number of official dinners at the base declined so much that a steak barbecue we had every Sunday on the officers' club patio became the highlight of our food service.

To maintain our combat readiness our company would periodically go out in the field, and several days beforehand, we of the general's mess would set up cooking and dining tents that sheltered all the grills, stoves, tables, and supplies that would be needed to support the troops during the field exercise. Once everything was set up, a guard was stationed at the mess site overnight.

During my stay in Korea we had to keep an eye on our friends in the south just as much as we did on the enemy in the north. On one memorable field exercise we arrived at the mess site early in the morning to begin food prep, and the guard was nowhere in sight. The captain in charge shouted out, asking where he was, and a bedraggled soldier slowly emerged from his tent, clad only in his skivvies. The captain asked him why he wasn't in uniform while the rest of us tried to keep from cracking up.

He had spent the night drinking and enjoying the services of a "slicky girl" (Korenglish for female thief), the guard confessed, and after she left, had crawled into his sleeping bag to sleep it off. While he slumbered the slicky girl stole back to the mess site, and with accomplices carted off as many of our pots and pans and other kitchen gear as they could carry, and—presumably so he wouldn't give chase if he woke up—the guard's uniform and boots. Earlier in the evening the slicky girl had relieved him of his wallet.

Normally you would get an "Article 15" for a caper like this, but after giving the guard a good ass chewing, the lieutenant let him off the hook, we guessed because he had only been "guarding" the mess site, and hadn't compromised the security of the whole company. The incident earned the guard the nickname "the Boxer Sentinel," which stuck the rest of the time I was in Korea.

The field exercises were supposed to be held on a moment's notice, but in fact we all knew when they were coming and were prepared well in advance of the actual sounding of the alarm.

As for the food prep, we didn't miss a beat. During the exercises we offered the same fare we had back on the base, even to the extent of placing flower arrangements on the tables for the evening meals, complimented by a wine service of Lancers and Mateus, popular Portuguese wines at that time. Except for the concertina wire and gun emplacements on the perimeter, you couldn't have dined better at the Waldorf.

The field exercises were the closest we ever got to the real thing, but none of us took them too seriously. Our free time was spent playing Pinochle and Hearts, and the card games often went on round the clock, with players coming and going at all hours.

When General Yarborough (the "Old Man") was still in command, we went all out for holiday dinners, and this is where my schooling allowed me to shine. In addition to the traditional salads, our holiday buffets featured such *garde manger* (cold kitchen) dishes as pâtes, fruit carvings, specialty seafood, and aspics (dishes in which the ingredients, usually meat, are set in gelatin made from meat stock), and *chaud froids*, similar to aspics, but with cream added to the meat stock.

Pulling off these culinary delights with the limited resources we had at the camp was quite an accomplishment for a 21-year old, fresh out of chef's school, I thought, patting myself on the back. Cooking for the general and visiting big wigs was a pretty big deal, too. I got cocky—but soon had my comeuppance, big time, at the most important VIP dinner we ever prepared: for Park Chung-hee, the then-president of South Korea.

President Park had come to power by a military coup in 1961, and ruled South Korea with an iron hand until he was assassinated in 1979. Despite his authoritarian rule, he is generally credited as being the architect of the "Miracle on the Han," the foundation of the economic powerhouse South Korea is today. (His daughter, Park Geun-hye, was elected South Korea's first female president in 2012.)

Only the top brass, Colonel Simons among them, would be attending the dinner for such an important personage, making it a much smaller and more intimate gathering than our usual VIP dinners.

When I met with General Yarborough to plan the dinner, we decided that beef brochettes skewered on military sabers and flamed table side would suitably impress our honored guest, given his military background. A presentation like this had never been attempted at the base before, and was sure to be a meal everyone would remember. And it was.

Flaming the brochettes involved a certain amount of showmanship. I was excited by the prospect of not only showing off my culinary skills, but winning an Oscar for this aspect of the presentation.

Wanting to look my best, I borrowed black dress shoes, black slacks and a black sport coat. I couldn't have weighed more than 150 pounds at the time, and the sport coat and slacks were much too big on me. So were the shoes, size 12, when I wore a size 9. Fortunately I didn't have to borrow a white dress shirt, as I had one, the only article of clothing that fit me. Not exactly the look of a model out of GQ magazine, but I would be standing behind a table, giving me some cover.

The service table was about the size of a card table, and not having a tablecloth that fit it, we covered the table top with paper doilies and placed the beautifully carved watermelon basket that would be the centerpiece of our presentation on the doilies.

The plan was to skewer cubes of filet mignon and fresh vegetables on four large military sabers of the kind Custer's men would have wielded at the battle of Little Big Horn. The brochettes and vegetables were to be skewered on the sabers and broiled in the kitchen, then delivered to me at the service table for flaming. A small lit candle was hidden in the bottom of the watermelon basket, and after dousing the sabers with Bacardi 151, a highly flammable rum, I would stab each rum-soaked saber into the basket. When it touched the candle flame, the rum would ignite and travel up from the tip of the saber to the handle.

The first saber lit perfectly. A light blue flame danced up and along the steak and vegetable-skewered blade, flickering for a second or two, and after it went out I slid the food bits off the saber with a chef's fork onto a platter for service, and set the saber aside.

I had soaked the remaining three sabers with rum when I coated the first one, and they were lying on a tray on the table waiting to be flamed. Unbeknownst to me, a small puddle of rum had formed under them.

I picked up the second saber and stabbed it into the watermelon basket, but it wouldn't light. I brushed it back and forth in the candle flame, but still no luck. The alcohol must have evaporated, I thought, and took the saber out of the basket to coat it with fresh rum. A small fatty piece of meat on the tip of the saber had in fact caught fire, but I didn't notice it smoldering when I put the saber down on the tray with the others so I could pick up the bottle of Bacardi and unscrew its cap.

The smoldering brochette was just hot enough to ignite the tray, which went up with a spectacular whoosh. All three sabers were suddenly ablaze, and worse yet, the make-shift table cloth of paper doilies caught fire. Instinctively, I swatted at the doilies in a frantic effort to put them out, burning my hand and setting the sleeve of the baggy sport coat I was wearing on fire. An officer at one of the tables leaped up from his seat and yelled out for the safety NCO, but to no avail—doubling as the safety NCO was one of the duties I assumed when I was promoted to mess sergeant, a poor choice under the circumstances.

Ji-hu, one of our Korean nationals, was tending bar and came to my rescue by tossing me a bottle of seltzer, the kind powered by a CO_2 cartridge. With a short burst of no more seltzer than would fill a highball glass if you were making a gin fizz, I doused the flames that were licking at the elbow of my sport jacket, then aimed the seltzer bottle at the flaming doilies and held the trigger down, sending a torrent of carbonated water

ripping across the table top and ashes from the half-burned doilies flying everywhere. The blast put out the fire, but made such a mess we needed a mop-up crew to clean everything up.

Thoroughly dejected, I took the tray of sabers with the brochettes still attached into the kitchen to rework them on plates to finish the dinner. What a disaster. I had embarrassed my country in front of the most powerful man in South Korea, but I didn't think of it that way. I knew nothing about the man, but I did know General Yarborough and couldn't forget the gleam in his eyes as we sat together in his office planning this night. I couldn't face him now.

With the dinner served, I left the kitchen and retreated to the hooch I shared with four bunk mates, normally a refuge where you kicked back and had a beer. When I came in, "Bad Moon Rising" by Creedence Clearwater Revival was blaring on AFKN. I went over to my bunk, and after stripping off the ridiculous Charlie Chaplin outfit I had been wearing, I sat on my bunk in my skivvies and T-shirt and stared down at my hand, still red from the burn I'd received trying to put out the table fire.

"Ah-tenn-SHUN!" one of the guys suddenly shouted, and we all sprang to our feet as Colonel Bull Simons strode into the hooch.

"Cut that shit out," he snorted. "I'm here to see Gentieu."

This is it, I thought. I won't have to wait till morning to get my butt reamed.

Colonel Bull Simons was a soldier's soldier, as tough as nails, who, during and after his Army career, was involved in several rescue missions, missions as dangerous as they come. In World War II he had been part of the raiding party that freed survivors of the Bataan Death March from a Japanese POW camp in Luzon in the Philippines. During the Vietnam war, he led a mission to rescue American POWs from the Son Tay prison in North Vietnam. A man of few words, he never beat around the bush.

"Gentieu, I want to tell you I've never had better beef brochettes than I had tonight," he said in his familiar gruff voice.

I was stunned.

"Tender as a mother's love. With just the right touch of seltzer," Colonel Simons grinned as he patted me on the shoulder. "And don't worry about the Old Man. Best damn brochettes he ever had too. Even better than the Soufflé Potatoes," the colonel said with a wink, before turning to leave. "You'll do fine in your chef's career when your tour's up."

As I said, he was a man of few words.

After his retirement from the Army, Colonel Simons organized a mission for Ross Perot that freed two of his employees held hostage in Iran. Sadly, he passed away shortly after that, in 1979, at the age of 60. It was an honor and a privilege to have served with him at Camp Red Cloud, and I'll never forget the night he came into my lowly hooch to cheer me up after the worst day in my two years in the army.

CHAPTER 8

THE DAY FROM HELL:
Wet Pants and Other Distractions

I reached my office on that May morning with yet another cup of coffee in my hand. The way things were going it was time for some positive self-talk, something I relied on when faced with stress-inducing problems of the kind we were experiencing. "I am the best, I can do it, and I like myself," I repeated over and over in the privacy of my office, giving my attitude and energy level much-needed boosts. Coffee gulped and batteries charged, I began making the morning calls.

The ad copy had to be handled, chicken breasts had to be located, a locksmith had to be called to extract the broken key from the change drawer, the menu for the Kiwanis group had to be set, and I still had to figure out how to solve the two most important problems: 1) how we were now going to handle two parties that were starting in a couple of hours while so short-staffed? And 2) where was I going to get another pair of pants? Mine were completely drenched.

Right when I was about to pick up the phone and call Midge to shoot down with a fresh pair, the intercom crackled. A lady and her daughter wanted to see me about something. Experience told me this could be anything from needing a job for the daughter to sponsoring the rodeo queen.

In the 20 years I'd been in the restaurant business by this point, barely a day went by without someone (or some organization) hitting me up for a donation of some kind. It was either an outright request for money, or one of the following: free dinners, food donations, catering help, sponsoring this or that worthy cause, advertising in the local paper, or signing up to be in a coupon book.

I'm all for supporting community events and helping where I can. But I've learned that once you give, folks return time and again. Donation requests are so frequent that if we gave to everyone who stopped by, no profit would be left for the business.

44

Usually, the person seeking a donation stops by with no appointment and goes right into his or her pitch, completely insensitive to how busy I might be at any given moment. The worst offenders drop in at lunch, clueless as to how inconvenient it is for me. And, believe it or not, it sometimes comes as a real news flash that, like other businesses, we're there to make a profit.

"I just finished lunch," begins the classic approach. "The food was great, as usual, and by the way we're having an event you may want to sponsor."

Whether or not I contribute often has less to do with the worthiness of any particular cause than with what's going on at the time I'm asked, the mood I'm in when a request is made, and the type of request that's made. And, though I hate to admit it, if it's a pretty lady making the pitch, the chances for a positive result greatly increase.

What works best for us is to let a person know we have a yearly budget for giving and that requests should be submitted in writing. This eliminates about 90 percent of the donation requests that come our way, since most folks are just too lazy to complete this one reasonable step. And it frees us up to seriously consider the remaining 10 percent. If you want something from a restaurant, make your approach professional. We can handle that.

Because our business was in a small town, we made every effort to meet our customers' needs and requests. Customers were always Numero Uno at Leonard's, and treating them that way meant repeat business. Plus it always made a customer feel special to speak to the owner, so out I went.

"Hi, I'm Leonard. What can I do for you?" I asked the lady, who obviously wasn't seeking employment for her daughter, who couldn't have been more than two years old. For openers, the lady began telling me how much she and her family enjoyed eating at the restaurant and how they recommended it to all their friends at every opportunity. I thanked her for that, and mentally prepared myself for the close. It turned out that Little Suzy had been entered in the Little Miss Whatever-it-Was Beauty Contest, and needed sponsorship to be able to attend the pageant. I couldn't imagine that there could be a beauty contest for two-year olds, but asked what being a sponsor meant. What I wanted to know was how much this was going to cost me.

Sponsorship, the lady explained, required purchasing one or more raffle tickets for a trip to Cancun (four days, three nights, great food, sandy white beaches as far as the eye could see, the whole bit). "How much are the tickets and how soon is the plane leaving?" I asked the lady.

"Twenty-five dollars apiece, or five for $100," mom answered.

Opening my wallet, I pulled out a twenty-dollar bill and a five, and signed up. I had just invested $25 in two-year old Suzy's future, and it would take the sale of 50 hamburgers to generate the profit needed to recoup that investment. Such expenditures are usually listed on the monthly Profit and Loss statement as "Promotions" or "Advertising." The thought crossed

my mind that there really should be two more categories for this type of expense—"Just Lost my Head" and "Easy Touch."

Back in the office, I took time out to check the day's mail. I always enjoyed going through the mail to see what corporate receivables were being paid, and if we had received any thank-you notes from customers telling us how much they liked our food and service. When I started out in the restaurant business I thrived on accolades, and that was even more true when I became an owner and learned how much effort it takes to make a restaurant work.

Today's mail was a mixed bag, a few bills, a few payment checks and an unemployment claim—and a trade magazine featuring an article entitled, "Stress and Today's Business Owner." It made me laugh. What timing!

A knock on the office door interrupted mail call. "C'mon in," I said, and when the door opened I was greeted by a fire service technician wanting to inspect our exhaust hood system and hand-held fire extinguishers. Each year a service tech checks to make sure the hood system is operational and the extinguishers are fully charged. If any deficiencies are found, they must be remedied immediately, and that can be expensive, especially if the deficiency involves the exhaust hood. After the inspections, none of which we'd ever failed, we paid the inspection fee and had our fire prevention equipment tagged, "Good for another year." Distracted by all the things that had been going wrong, I'd forgotten the inspection had been scheduled for today.

Seeing the door open, Gloria poked her head in to tell me the rep from the paper had called again, asking where the ad copy was. "Be a doll and fax her a copy of the menu. She'll know what to do with it," I instructed Gloria, hopefully disposing of that problem.

Sensing that we were having a hectic day, the fire service tech offered to reschedule the inspection, but the only good time for that would have been after closing. Unfortunately, fire inspections aren't performed late at night. "Can you complete the inspection before lunch gets under way?" I asked.

"No problem," the tech smiled, "in 45 minutes all your equipment will be tagged and you'll have a full report on your desk." Just what I needed—a report on my desk!

Leonard's was so much more complex and challenging to operate than my first sandwich shop, Gentieu's Pantry. The operation of the Pantry was a walk in the park compared to where I was now. And we hadn't even hit lunch.

DAY FROM HELL

Tools of the Trade

The classic French knife is the most important, most used tool in the kitchen. If you like to cook and don't have a high-quality French knife, get one and learn to use it. The more you work with it, the more proficient you'll become.

My favorite is a 12-inch Pro "S" French Knife by Zwilling J.A. Henckels, a German knife manufacturer. I have had it several years and found it versatile and extremely durable. It's excellent for cutting steaks from New York strips, rib eyes, and top block sirloins, and the 12-inch blade provides more leverage for chopping. It enables a straight, smooth slice through large cuts of meat, works well on whole chickens, and handles as a knife should for filleting salmon, splitting lobsters, and cutting cabbage chiffonade. In fact, a good French knife can carry out most of the cutting tasks a kitchen requires.

Serious cooks will also need a good serrated bread knife, a boning knife, and a paring knife.

When I began my career, the best knives were made by German manufacturers that had been around for centuries—companies like Henckels, founded in 1731. French-made knives by Sabatier were also popular. Their knives featured a full tang, which means the blade goes all the way through the handle to the end of the grip, still a quality feature to look for.

More recently, Japanese knives have become available to chefs and are also very popular. Japanese knives are light, super sharp, well-balanced and comfortable to use. Top manufacturers include Shun, Kyocera, Global, and Mac, which is endorsed by Chefs Thomas Keller and Eric Ribert.

The Dexter Russell Company, founded in Massachusetts in 1818, is the largest American cutlery manufacturer. Dexter's French Knife has been a workhorse in commercial kitchens for decades, and most chefs have Dexter oyster and clam knives. The brand is a very cost-effective alternative to more expensive imports, although many chefs question its ability to hold a sharp edge.

A certain amount of prestige accompanies use of the latest, greatest, costliest imported knife. However, a skilled knife handler can get the job done with almost any blade, as long as it's sharp. Owning the right knife is very much a question of personal preference but, more important, a matter of how well it's maintained.

Properly tended, a knife will last years. It may seem obvious, but the most important maintenance is to keep the edge sharp. A dull knife is not only harder to use but less safe, as it requires more pressure to cut, and tends to slide off the food as more pressure is applied.

Here are some things not to do with a knife. DON'T leave it in the kitchen sink, clean it in a dishwasher, or use it to cut on metal, ceramic, or granite surfaces; don't scrape foods from a cutting board using the sharp edge of the blade; and never try to catch a knife falling off the counter. Just let it fall.

On the other hand, DO clean a knife after each use by washing with a soapy cloth with the sharp edge facing away and rinsing with hot water; do store the knife wrapped in a clean towel or sheath so the blade is not touching other blades; and do keep it dry or, in humid climates, rubbed with a little mineral oil. Always chop on wood, plastic, or composite cutting boards, regularly use a steel to bring up the cutting edge, and sharpen it as needed on an oil or water stone (not an electric grinding wheel) or have it sharpened professionally.

CHAPTER 9

The First Deli

"Cheese steaks are the gastronomic icons of this ethnic city."

— Bryan Miller, on Philadelphia

Having grown up in Claymont, Delaware, about 25 miles from Philadelphia, the Philly Cheesesteak was part of my everyday life. Every deli and restaurant that served hot sandwiches offered its version of this "gastronomic icon." It wasn't a novelty or anything particularly special, it just was. But when I was getting ready to open Gentieu's Pantry in 1973 and was planning the menu, I discovered that the folks in Taft had no idea what a Philly Cheesesteak was. I sensed an opportunity. But I'm getting ahead of myself.

If ever there was an oil town, Taft, California, was it. Situated on the southwestern edge of the San Joaquin Valley in Kern County, thirty miles southwest of Bakersfield, its economy has depended on petroleum for its entire one hundred-year-plus history; in particular, it relies on the Midway-Sunset field, one of the country's largest. Since its discovery in 1894, Midway-Sunset has produced over three billion barrels of oil, and has about 500 million barrels still to be tapped. At one time, about two thirds of Taft's 9,000 residents worked in this and the neighboring Buena Vista field—another "super-giant," as fields of this size are called in the oil business.

How Taft got its name is a story in itself. According to local legend, the town was known only as "Siding Number Two on the Sunset Railroad" after the Southern Pacific laid its rails there in the 1890s. When the local people petitioned the railroad officials to change the name of the station to "Morro," the officials, fearing that "Morro" would be confused with nearby Morro Bay, chose "Moron" instead. Once the gaffe was realized, the name was quickly changed to Taft, in honor of President William Howard Taft.

Kathy (my first wife) and I wound up in Taft after my honorable discharge from the Army in 1970. Prior to our arrival there, a whole series of events took place and, as fate would have it, we were destined to land there. The journey began during the height of the Viet Nam war. Most of the men in my outfit were sent to Fort Polk, Louisiana, for combat training at Tigerland, so named for its resemblance to the jungles of southeast Asia. From there, they were shipped out to Vietnam. I, on the other hand, was sent to Fort Ord, near Monterey, before shipping out to Korea.

Like me, most of the guys in my outfit at basic training were draftees. None of us had volunteered for anything—the first rule of military service for draftees—but now all of us were headed to Asia. We were going to different places, but they had one thing in common: I didn't know why we were in either place. I didn't question it at the time, I just assumed that because I was being sent there by my country, it must be right. Unlike most of my boot camp brethren headed to Vietnam, the shooting war was long since over by the time I arrived in Korea. There were occasional incursions from the North across the DMZ, but most of the time it was quiet. And although I didn't receive a hero's welcome when I returned home, I didn't suffer the shameful treatment our Vietnam veterans did when they returned home.

I was very surprised not to be joining everyone else in Vietnam but clearly my Army time was born under a lucky star, and Korea was just more proof. The first piece of evidence came with my assignment to Fort Ord.

The second rule of Army service for draftees says, basically, that whatever you're qualified to do in civilian life will not be put to good use in the military. If you have a PhD in physics, you will be assigned the job of potato peeler in the mess hall instead of plotting the trajectories of artillery shells out on the gunnery range. That meant, if everything went like it was supposed to, I was going to be scouring intelligence reports my entire tour (I was severely dyslexic). But lady luck smiled on me, and the rule didn't apply. At Fort Ord, not only was I assigned to the unit that did the baking for the base, but part of my duties took me off site.

In partnership with California's Regional Occupational Programs (ROP), my unit helped provide vocational training in food service in the local high schools. When the captain in charge saw I was a graduate of Brown Tech and the CIA (the other CIA), he arranged for me to give cooking demonstrations to the students in nearby Salinas, where I quickly discovered that the food service program offered by ROP was nowhere near as advanced as the vocational training I'd received at Brown Tech.

Now *there* was a school. The motto that greeted you when you came through the entrance on 14th Street in Wilmington: "A person who works with his hands is a laborer. A person who works with his hands and mind is a craftsman. And a person who works with his hands, mind, and heart is an artisan and a Brown Vocational graduate."

The hands, mind, and heart I put into my cooking demos impressed the superintendent of schools in Salinas so much that he offered me a job heading up the food service program in one of them. He even petitioned the Army to give me an early out so I could take it. That didn't happen—nobody is that lucky—but the superintendent kept my home address and phone number on file, and that simple act was to have a profound effect on my future.

Duty at Fort Ord was the best you could get, and I only wished my stay there could have been longer. The base was named after Major General Edward Ord, who, with General Sheridan's cavalry, defeated Lee in the battle that ended the Civil War by forcing Lee to surrender at Appomattox Court House on April 9, 1865. Though my great-grandfather fought in many battles under General Sheridan, his regiment wasn't under General Sheridan's command at that time (it's believed to have been in North Carolina), thus he didn't witness this historic event.

Fort Ord was within walking distance of Monterey Bay, and only a mile or so from the town of Monterey, a haven for artists and home to many marine attractions, including the Monterey Bay Aquarium and a smaller version of San Francisco's Fisherman's Wharf. Cannery Row, made famous by John Steinbeck, who was born in Salinas, was another attraction. The weather was great, and on just about any day of the week you could see the sea otters frolicking out in the Bay and sea lions sprawled on the many wharves, sunning themselves. To someone whose first experience traveling had come from being drafted into the army, it was like encountering a new world. I bonded with the sea, and after Monterey, it became a part of me, just like my love of cooking.

Kathy and I had gotten married in 1966, and while I was in Korea she moved back into the apartment we had rented in Claymont. Like many couples starting out, we wanted to buy a house, but couldn't afford to, and resigned ourselves to apartment living. When I returned stateside from Korea, the plan was for me to go back to the DuPont Country Club where I'd worked prior to getting drafted, and for us to save up as much as we could. That's when yet another fortuitous surprise came winging out of the blue.

One afternoon I received a phone call from a man named Clyde Johnson, calling to offer me a job setting up and teaching a food service program at a high school, in Maricopa, California. Mr. Johnson was the superintendent of the Maricopa School District and I'd been recommended to him by the superintendent in Salinas who had offered me a similar job when I was at Fort Ord. I was hesitant—we were 2500 miles across the country, after all—but when Clyde offered to fly east to meet me in person, I took him up on it.

To save him making a trip to Claymont, we met at the Philadelphia Airport, truly an unusual place to hold a job interview. We went over the program I was to develop and what my teaching duties and salary would be. A certificate was needed before you could teach in California, but my CIA diploma and work experience, plus a crash course in teaching techniques at UCLA, would be an acceptable substitute.

I had never heard of Maricopa, and when I asked Clyde to tell me a little bit about it he launched into a Chamber-of-Commerce spiel, complete with brochures, extolling its scenic wonders. No, it wasn't exactly on the ocean like Monterey, he said, it was nestled in the foothills of the majestic Coast Range mountains, the "gateway to the sea," he called them, and yes, some parts of the San Joaquin Valley were desert-like, but Maricopa wasn't one of them. Nosiree. Why, pine trees even grew there, he assured me, and pointed to one in a photo in the glossy brochure he had brought along for the interview.

It would be a big step, picking up stakes and leaving the job I had. I'd have to think about it and talk it over with Kathy before I committed myself. I shook hands with Clyde when the interview was over, and promised to let him know my decision as soon as I could.

If all I had to consider was which of the two was the more desirable to live in, Claymont or California, the decision would have been a no brainer. But giving up my job at the DuPont Country Club made the decision much harder. I was the fourth generation of Gentieus to work for DuPont, and leaving would break that family tradition. Plus, they were my ticket to fulfilling my dream of becoming a chef and had held up their end of the bargain to keep me on and train me after returning from service. And besides, I didn't have any training as a teacher. What if I wasn't any good at it, or didn't like it? That part of the decision really ate at me.

Kathy's main concern was Maricopa. Not to worry, I assured her. It wasn't exactly like Monterey, and yes, some parts of the San Joaquin Valley were desert-like, but not Maricopa. Nosiree. Pine trees even grew there. See for yourself, I told Kathy, and handed her the glossy brochure Clyde left with me.

With these glowing assurances, she was on board, and left the decision to accept Clyde's offer up to me. Like "percentages," the one-word precept I would later follow in running my restaurants, the decision came down to one word: California. Then, as now, it was where you went if you wanted to escape where you were. It was a place of boundless opportunity and scenic wonder that I had seen first hand. The teaching job would get me there, and once there, I could renew my dream of becoming a chef and starting my own restaurant.

The people at the DuPont Country Club were great about it. They even gave me a going-away party. With that as a send-off, in August 1970, Kathy and I set out for Maricopa, nestled in the foothills of the majestic Coast Range Mountains, gateway to the sea.

With U-Haul in tow, we drove non-stop and arrived three days later on the outskirts of Taft, about seven miles north of Maricopa. With no stop lights to slow us down, we zipped through downtown Taft in no time flat. Maricopa would be seriously bigger, I assured Kathy, who did not miss the fact that there were no traffic lights. There would be much more to do there, too, we could count on that, but our first objective was to find a motel to rest up in and escape the 100 degree heat.

Matching the temperature, Maricopa turned out to be flat and desert-like land. The closest pine trees were twenty-five miles away in a grove on Mt. Pinos, the highest peak in nearby Ventura County, so high it was snow-covered for a good part of the year. On a clear day, with a telescope, you might be able to see the Pacific Ocean 100 miles away.

With a population of just over 1,000, Maricopa consisted of the high school, a gas station, the Maricopa Inn, and Gusher Hall where town meetings were held—its colorful name a reminder of the importance of oil to the town's economy, just as it is to Taft's. The outskirts of both towns were dotted with "grasshoppers" (the walking beams that pump the oil out of the ground), and a huge gas flare from one of the wells greeted us as we rolled into Maricopa.

Kathy took one look and was ready to flee back east. To tell the truth, I was too, but I had signed a contract, and was duty bound to honor it, which I did. I had taken the job with the understanding that teaching was not likely to be something I would spend the rest of my life doing, and the school was okay with that. Setting up the program and getting it off to a good start justified their investment in me, and everybody wished me well when I set out to open Gentieu's Pantry three years later.

I modeled Gentieu's Pantry after the sandwich shops I had known on the East Coast, offering a menu of their most popular sandwiches. Three kinds of sub (known as a "hoagie" in Philadelphia): turkey, tuna, and Italian, made with lettuce, tomato and onions with boiled ham and provolone and your choice of hard salami or capicolla; an Italian meatball sandwich and a double-decker hamburger on a French roll topped with coleslaw; and of course, a Philly cheese steak, the mainstay of any East Coast sandwich shop worth its salt.

Today, that sounds entirely normal. But in 1973, our sandwiches would be completely new to the area. (Capicolla? Does he play for the Dodgers?) With so much uncertainty, I made sure to market-test the sandwiches. Kathy and I invited several friends over to the home we rented and let them sample away. Surprisingly, our tasting team was puzzled by the Philly cheesesteak. I knew most of them had never heard of it before, but I figured they would at least know what to expect. I was wrong. They had expected it to be a thick cut of meat served open-face on a slice of sourdough, not grilled thinly-sliced beef over fried onions topped with cheese (purists will insist on Cheese Whiz). Fortunately, they loved it and all the other subs, which was a great surprise considering they were all new to their palates. Everyone encouraged me to open the sandwich shop.

I leased a 900-square-foot storefront near the center of Taft for $300 a month and, purchased a deli case for the bargain price of $100 from a local market that had closed. The balance of the equipment—a stove, grill, a fryer, a maple-topped table and a commercial refrigerator and various kitchenware—was purchased in Los Angeles for $7,000 scraped together from our savings and credit card advances. Compared to what I would later spend in opening Leonard's, this was pennies.

Working long hours into the night, with the help of friends, we were able to get everything set up in less than a week. Except for the rolls, all the ingredients I needed were available locally. Since our fare consisted entirely of sandwiches, the rolls were critically important. So important, in fact, I'd shipped them in by air from Philadelphia for the market testing. That, of course, would not be feasible for supplying the sandwich shop.

Going outside Taft to find an alternative, I discovered a bakery in Bakersfield that was able to duplicate the rolls exactly. Its name: the Pyrénées French Bakery. This source of exactly the right rolls was so essential to our success I arranged to have the rolls transported to Gentieu's Pantry daily via the bus service between Taft and Bakersfield.

After hiring a staff of two and placing a "Grand Opening" ad in the Midway Driller, the local paper named after the Midway-Sunset field, we were ready for business. My journey as an entrepreneur had begun.

Starting up, my management style was to fly by the seat of my pants. In our first year, we grossed over $100,000, not a huge sum, but we were solidly profitable. Quickly I learned that to run a successful business, even one as small as a sandwich shop, overseeing every aspect of the business yourself is essential.

CHAPTER 10

THE DAY FROM HELL:
Not the Toilets! Yes, and More!

As the fire inspector went to get his equipment for the inspection, I looked up to see Albert standing in the doorway with a dripping toilet plunger in his hand. Clearly he was not bringing good news.

"What's the problem?" I asked.

"Both the restrooms are backed up," came the answer.

"Did you put up the 'Out of Order' signs?"

"Did that first thing."

"How long did you spend trying to clear the blockage?"

"About fifteen minutes, and the toilets still won't flush."

A quick look in the restrooms left little doubt that we had a major blockage. I'll spare the details, except to say I'd rather have repaired the dishwasher all over again. For this one, we'd need professional help.

I went back to the office, and while I was scanning the Rolodex for the plumber's number the intercom brought the news that the floor sinks in the kitchen had backed up too, and water was everywhere.

Tiptoeing into the flooded kitchen and soaking my Bally's again, I confirmed my worst fear. The blockage obviously involved more than the rest room drains. There had to be a blockage in the main line and our location at the far end of the shopping center was at the end of the line. I instructed Albert to turn off the dishwasher, grab a busboy and start squeegeeing the water out the back door. Meanwhile my mind raced ahead to the lunch hour. Two parties totaling 75 people were heading our way, and I had not yet nailed down the menu for one of them, we had a shortage of servers, a fire inspector on the premises and a plumbing backup that, if not fixed soon, would necessitate equipping the line cooks with snorkels.

I forced myself to focus on the most urgent problem—the blocked drain. Benjamin's Plumbing was the only plumber in town, and I went back to the office and quickly dialed his number. His wife answered and said that Ben was on a service call at the Navy Reserve base north of town.

DAY
FROM
HELL

"Listen, I've got a serious drain blockage at the restaurant. Can you reach him?" I pleaded. "It's an emergency." She said she would try, a response I've found almost never leads to a successful outcome. My problem was more important to me than it was to her, and since patience has never been one of my virtues and the water in the kitchen was still rising, I waited a minute, then called the Navy Reserve base myself. With two calling, surely one of us would get through to Ben of Benjamin's Plumbing.

"Navy Reserve, can you hold?" the receptionist asked me politely. Having no other option, I held.

"Sorry to keep you waiting, what extension please?" the receptionist asked after five seemingly endless minutes of elevator music.

"I don't know the extension, but would you happen to know what department Benjamin's Plumbing is working in?"

"That's funny," the receptionist answered in a puzzled voice, "you're the second person who's tried to reach him in the last few minutes. Is this some kind of emergency?" It definitely was, one that absolutely couldn't wait, I assured her.

"I'll connect you to Maintenance," she responded, and with a sickening click, the phone went dead.

No time to lose my cool, though, and I quickly dialed the number of the Navy Reserve base again.

"Navy Reserve, can you hold please?"

Is it just me? Or has anyone on earth called someone working for a government agency and gotten through on the first try?

"How may I direct your call?"

I spoke quickly, disguising my voice so the receptionist wouldn't know it was me calling again, and asked for the Maintenance Department.

"Thank you."

This time the call miraculously went through, and a man's cheerful voice answered. "Maintenance, Larry." I identified myself and was explaining that I had an emergency and needed to talk to Ben of Benjamin's Plumbing when Larry was suddenly called away from the phone. When he returned he resumed our conversation with "Ben who?" Ben the plumber, you idiot! I wanted to scream. Can't you tell it's an emergency?

"I'm trying to get hold of Ben of Benjamin's Plumbing," I said as calmly as I could. "He has a gig at the base today. Have you seen him?"

"There's a guy working on the showers for the office girls' volleyball team," Larry answered.

"That must be him. Can you get him for me?"

"I'll try and transfer you."

Another sickening click. Sure enough, we had been disconnected.

I couldn't waste any more time tracking down Ben, and went back to the kitchen to assess the situation and craft a new plan. Albert and the busboy were barely keeping up with the water, and it was about to breach the threshold of the kitchen doors leading to the dining room. Soiled aprons were quickly packed around the doors to staunch the flow.

Despite the plumbing crisis, the fire inspection was on track, with the inspector returning from his truck outfitted in black rubber boots and toting a ladder to inspect the upper area of the exhaust hood. I couldn't help thinking how ironic it was that someone should be inspecting for fire hazards in what might soon be a flood zone.

Even though I would be perfectly justified in crying, I began to laugh. The inspector, the only dry person in the kitchen, was making sure the hood system could contain a conflagration while the rest of us were soaked and trying to keep the home fires burning, among them the tilt skillet's pilot light, which was in danger of being put out again from the still-rising water.

Having had no luck with Benjamin's Plumbing, I had to find another plumber, even if from out of town—and soon. As I scanned the yellow pages my right eyelid began to twitch, making everything on the pages jump up and down. I tried more positive self-talk. "Relax, stay calm, think soothing thoughts," I told myself, "you're okay, settle down, breathe slowly."

Chicken breasts! The words flashed across my mind like a thunderbolt. We still didn't have any for the baby shower, and lunch was looming. After several frantic calls, I finally located two cases at a local grocery. Even though they were the wrong size, and buying them at retail increased my cost about 25 percent, we simply had to have them.

Knowing the chicken breasts were on their way calmed my twitching eye, but that was quickly replaced by itching feet. My soaked shoes and socks had triggered a wicked flare-up of athlete's foot. Usually I could control the itching by rubbing one foot on top of the other, but this attack was heavy duty, requiring the removal of both shoes and socks. Rubbing a towel between my wet, shriveled-up toes felt great but there was no time to keep scratching.

I replaced my dress socks with a pair of white sport socks from the bottom drawer of the office file cabinet. Combined with my dark slacks and black shoes, they didn't make much of a fashion statement, but at least they were dry.

As I slipped on my shoes, the intercom brought the news that the plumber had arrived. "Mazel tov!" I shouted, as Bernie Goldman, our neighbor in the strip mall, would have shouted upon hearing the news. Ben's wife must have gotten through after all. Help had arrived, and I rushed into the kitchen.

"Benjamin, you don't know how glad I am to see you! Do we ever have a problem!"

"C-c-call me B-B-Ben."

Ben, as I was now permitted to call him, was a great guy, and I didn't think any less of him because of the stuttering, but it did slow our communication down. Time was of the essence, as the lunch hour (and the parties in the banquet rooms) would soon be upon us. I started to explain what the trouble was when Ben interrupted.

"D-d-do y-y-you have a blueprint of the p-p-plumbing p-p-plan?"

"Do we absolutely have to have the blueprint to find the blockage?" I

DAY FROM HELL

56

asked, thinking the blueprint was buried away somewhere in the store room and would take forever to find. With a look of dismay on his face, Ben slowly shook his head from side to side while his lips made an odd sucking sound.

I had seen that look before, dealing with workers in the building trades. How well I remembered the electrician who looked at our service panel during a remodeling job. He exhibited the same body language, right down to the lip sucking. He wasn't sure whether the kind of breakers we needed were still available, or that they would carry our electrical load, and how was he ever going to run new lines to our location anyway?

And I remembered the carpenter who complained that the original builder hadn't made the walls square or the floor level. He had issues with the fire wall, too, and there were problems with the load-bearing walls and the door headers, not to mention all the new building codes that had to be complied with.

Having been through several restaurant start-ups, I had a good deal of insight into the meaning of Ben's body language. I understood how difficult the job would be, I assured Ben, and how relieved I was that he was here, and that if anyone could get the job done, he could, even without the blueprint, and when he did get the job done he was going to be my hero. All we had to do was get started.

CHAPTER 11

Gentieu's Gigantic, Gastronomical Delight

"You need a little bit of insanity to do great things."

— Henry Rollins

"Thank you for your letter enclosing the authentication for the 464.04 foot loaf and sandwich of a similar length which you have succeeded in producing," read the response from Guinness Superlatives. "This very fine specimen does, of course, overtake the 400 foot 6¾-inch production baked at the Boise State University, Idaho, and is the new record holder. Your record will appear in the 15th edition of the Guinness Book of World Records. Our congratulations."

Mission accomplished! In October, 1975, we'd made the world's longest sandwich and Guinness's letter made it official.

The grandiose grinder was headlined in the Midway Driller as "Gentieu's Gigantic, Gastronomical Delight," and was the highlight of Oildorado Days, a ten-day event held every five years in Taft to celebrate its oil history, a history that began with a bang in March 1910 with the eruption of the Lakeview Gusher between Taft and Maricopa. Before it was brought under control, the Lakeview Gusher became the country's largest oil spill, dwarfing even the Deepwater Horizon spill in the Gulf of Mexico, and how it happened is a story in itself.

The Lakeview Oil Company was founded in 1909 by Julius Fried, a former grocery salesman, to explore for oil in the area surrounding the Buena Vista Lake in Kern County. Legend has it that on the advice of a mysterious and nameless old-timer, the company purchased a patch of land covered by red grass, purportedly a sign of oil below, in what later became the Buena Vista field.

2 Cecil Court, London Road
Enfield, Middlesex EN2 6DJ
Telephone : 01 366 4551
Telegrams and cables : MOSTEST ENF

Guinness Superlatives Limi
A MEMBER OF THE GUINNESS GROUP OF CO
PUBLISHERS

6th November, 1975.

Mr. L. W. Gentieu,
Gentieu's Pantry,
231 North Street,
Taft,
California,
U.S.A.

Dear Mr. Gentieu,

Thank you for you letter dated 21st October enclosing the authenti for the 464.04 foot loaf and sandwich of a similar length which y succeeded in producing at Bakersfield.

This very fine specimen does of course overtake the 400 ft. 6¾ in baked at the Boise State University, Idaho, and is the new record

Your letter together with the notarized statement and newspaper have been placed with the papers which will be before the edit next revision period. Provided that your fine effort is not ov meantime it will appear in the 15th edition of the Guinness Boo Records in October 1976.

Please give our congratulations to all concerned in this fine With all best wishes,

Yours sincerely

N. Blason

G. HOWARD GARRARD
Correspondence Editor
Guinness Book of Records

After more than a year of unproductive drilling conducted by Lakeview's aptly named foreman, Charlie "Dry Hole" Woods, the company ran into financial difficulty, and was acquired by Union Oil, who wanted to use the site to store natural gas and directed that drilling cease. The drilling crew disobeyed and struck oil at 2,200 feet. The resultant gusher shot 200 feet in the air, and was so powerful it destroyed the drilling rig.

It spouted uncontrolled for a year and a half, spewing as much as 100,000 barrels of oil a day. The lake of oil it formed was so large, people crossed it in boats. By the time the well collapsed of its own accord in September 1911, about 9 million barrels of oil had been released, of which less than half was recovered, the rest having either soaked into the ground or evaporated. Even so, the amount recovered was so huge it cut the price of oil in half, to about 30 cents a barrel.

Today, a plaque marks the spot where the gusher erupted, which except for a few scattered patches of asphalt, is indistinguishable from the barren land that surrounds it (the site can be viewed on YouTube by typing "Lakeview Gusher" in the search bar).

The Oildorado Days held in October 1975 commemorated the 65th anniversary of Taft's founding as "Taft," having been known as the ill-chosen "Moron" prior to 1910. As the owner of Gentieu's Pantry, then only two years in business, I wanted to contribute to the festivities which included parades and many other events, including a best beard contest for the men, and of course, plenty of food for all.

The celebration provided an opportunity for good publicity. Several universities across the country had been pursuing the record for the world's longest sandwich, and that gave me the idea to enter the race as part of Taft's Oildorado celebration. It wasn't as dramatic as, say, chasing the world land-speed record at the Bonneville Salt Flats, but a challenge, nonetheless. Here we were, a small sandwich shop in a small town with scant resources—and we were going to compete and win. This was going to be my personal Olympics.

My plan was to create a sandwich 500 feet long, about 100 feet longer than the then-current record holder. To get an idea of just how long that would be, Cecil Walker, who would build our baking rack, and I, took a 500-foot roll of kite string and unwound it on Third Street where Gentieu's Pantry was located. That's when the reality of just how long 500 feet is sank in—almost the length of two football fields.

To qualify for the Guinness record, the loaf of bread would have to be baked in one continuous length with no breaks—we would not be allowed to cut the ends off of pre-baked loaves and line them up to make our length. That meant we would need an oven 500 feet long. Many ideas came to mind before I settled on baking the bread underground.

To make a test oven, no easy task in itself, a team of friends and myself dug a 5-foot trench in my backyard. We lined the bottom with charcoal to produce the heat for baking, and crafted an oven rack by tying chicken wire to steel rebar to make a cradle, which we lined with aluminum foil to hold the bread dough.

After lighting the coals and allowing them to burn down, we rolled out the dough and placed it in the cradle, then lowered the cradle into the make-shift oven and covered it with aluminum sheets. Twenty-five minutes later we retrieved a beautiful golden brown loaf of bread—all in one piece. Now all we had to do was make the length of the test oven 100 times longer.

For that we found a flat, vacant field about six blocks from the Pantry. Jim Kelley, a backhoe operator for an oilfield construction company, dug the trench while Cecil welded the 500-foot rebar rack. We wanted to get everything ready, including baking the loaf, on the Friday before the Saturday we planned to fill and sell the monster.

While driving that morning to the Pyrénées French Bakery in Bakersfield to pick up the bins of bread dough, a background piece on the 400 footer that had been made at Boise State University coincidentally came over the radio. That record won't stand for long, I chuckled. It's toast.

I brought back the dough and a crew of four French bakers from the bakery to roll the dough in pieces and join them together on long, wood-topped tables we'd set up parallel to the trench. Everything was going well until we reached the 460-foot mark, when the lead baker informed me were out of dough—the dough to extend the loaf the last 40 feet had been left behind on the mistaken assumption it was needed at the bakery.

This glitch almost precipitated a panic attack. I suddenly felt overwhelmed. There was so much yet to be done, and so many things that could go wrong. First, I had to coordinate the volunteers and time the lighting of the charcoal so it wouldn't burn down too fast and lose its heat before the dough was ready, then I had to supervise the rolling of the dough to give it enough time to proof (rise) before placing it into our subterranean oven for baking. And I needed to determine when to take it out so it would emerge as one continuous loaf. There would be no faking this with a notary and film crew on site.

The dough shortage would mean we would miss our 500-foot goal, but we were too far along to go back to the bakery and pick up the bin that had been left behind. The dough was rapidly proofing as we shaped the loaf, and would soon double in size. At 40 minutes, the round trip to Bakersfield would take too long, and I decided to go with what we had, and told Cecil to cut the last 36 feet off the rebar rack, downsizing it to 464 feet. We could still beat the record, if it all worked.

Keeping the loaf together was the most critical step. If it pulled apart, all our effort would have been for naught, and we would end up with pieces of a very long loaf that would keep us in sandwich bread for a very long time at Gentieu's Pantry. I was already worn out from the preparatory work and it

Gastronomical record set at 1975 Oildorado

Oildorado 1975 was known as much for its gastronomical feat as for the city's 75th anniversary.

Local restauranteur Leonard Gentieu decided the way to put Taft on the map was to do something really big.

It was. The sandwich, that is.

Gentieu's forte was sandwiches, but the one he created for the 1975 celebreation wasn't anything the regular Joe was going to find on the menu.

Gentieu set out to break the world record for the longest sandwich with a goal of 500 feet. A miscalculation in the ingredients had the massive meal come up a bit short, but the 464-foot total was still a record breaker.

Gentieu and a staff of 125 volunteers would work throughout the night baking the enormous loaf of bread needed to make one continuous sandwich.

A 500-foot oven was created out of what was then a vacant field on Fourth Street. A trench was created into which the dough was placed. Sheets of metal covered the top to complete the makeshift bakery.

Then the 464-foot loaf had to be transported -- undamaged. More than 100 Taft College students were enlisted to hoist the loaf in unison then carry it to a cordonned off section of Third Street between North and Center. There it was guarded throughout the night.

The following morning, the day of the Oildorado Grand Parade, Gentieu and his sandwich team went to work. The delicate job of slicing the loaf went without a hitch as Gentieu and helpers piled mountains of meats, lettuce and fresh vegetables onto the creation.

Once the record was certified, then-4th District Supervisor Vance Webb had the honor of cutting the first slice.

The sandwich

59

was still only Friday morning. We had another 24 hours to go, and the list of things that had to be done (and my stress level) increased by the hour.

Over half a ton of charcoal was needed to fill the trench that served as the oven, and several gallons of kerosene to light it. We primed the charcoal by having volunteers walk along the trench carrying punctured kerosene cans, then lit one end and watched as a bright red and yellow flame raced down the length of the trench in a matter of seconds. The whoosh reminded me of the flaming brochette incident I'd experienced at Camp Red Cloud, but obviously on a much greater scale.

Once the charcoal settled into a bed of glowing embers, on the count of three I called out on a bull horn and 100 students from Taft College lifted up the dough-filled rack, then eased it down into our backhoe-built oven and covered it with 300 tented aluminum sheets, formerly press plates, donated by the Midway Driller.

Twenty minutes later, at about 10 a. m., the gang of 100, potholders in hand, reached into the trench and pulled out a beautifully baked loaf of bread. A local notary and a County Supervisor verified not only the loaf's length, but that it was continuous, with no tears or separations. Students from the California Institute of the Arts in Valencia had filmed it as we baked. This was going to be the most well-documented event in the history of the world's largest sandwich competitions.

After letting the loaf cool, we sealed it in cellophane to prepare it for the six-block, 20-minute trip to Gentieu's Pantry. Riding along in a city patrol car, I called out cadence over the bull horn to the Taft One Hundred, to keep everyone in step, like a drill sergeant.

Moving along like a huge centipede, the giant loaf was a genuinely bizarre sight. The route was lined with spectators who gawked and pointed as the loaf inexorably approached its destination amid the party atmosphere that prevailed. Our police escort stopped traffic on Route 33, the main highway through town, to allow the behemoth to cross, and I could only imagine what unknowing drivers must have thought (WTF? comes to mind) as they watched the seemingly endless loaf pass by.

When we reached the Pantry, we heaved the humongous hoagie roll up, then carefully set it down atop a two-block row of sixty-five highway barricades put up in the center of the street. And that's where we left it— wrapped, unsliced and guarded through the night.

The night passed uneventfully, save for a drunk who, upon encountering the loaf, fled to the nearest bar, despite being assured he wasn't hallucinating.

On Saturday, the day of the event, I awoke at 4 a. m. to cut the huge loaf in half along its entire length. Just this simple step took an hour. As soon as I finished, and still before sunrise, the assembly team lifted the top half of our super-sub off the bottom half and began layering the 450-pound roll with two gallons of Spanish olive oil, 400 lbs. of salami, 300 lbs. of ham, 200 lbs. of cheese, six crates each of lettuce and tomatoes, 50 lbs. of onions, 3,000 "pepperoncini" dilled peppers, and 12 gallons of pickles. Then we carefully folded the top back over our heroic hero. Final weight: well over half a ton.

Next, the assembly team cut the tabletop torpedo into 3,000 slices, each about 2 inches long, to be sold for a dollar per slice. I waved to the crew atop Gentieu's Pantry to release the two thousand or so helium-filled balloons assembled under a parachute that would signal to one and all that the world's largest sandwich could now be consumed, precipitating a stampede that accomplished just that in less than 30 minutes, possibly setting another Guinness record in the process.

I later learned that some people took their slices home and stored them in their freezers as mementos. One couple even brought me a slice ten years later, and asked me if I would like a bite. I respectfully declined.

Early on, we selected Taft's non-profit West Side Training Center to be the recipient of the sandwich proceeds. The Center provided wonderful and badly needed services to Taft's special needs citizens, and it was my pleasure to present a check for over $1,600 to Janet Fishburn, the Center's administrator. Upon receiving it, she asked me if I had any ideas as to how the funds might best be used. I suggested taking everyone to Disneyland for a day, and she agreed it was a great idea.

Afterwards, the Center presented me with a homemade poster filled with pictures showing all the fun everyone had. It was the nicest "thank you" I've ever received, and I still have and cherish it to this day.

Our Great Sandwich Adventure proved to be a boon to business. When Gentieu's Pantry re-opened the following Monday, sales doubled. And the publicity was the kind you just can't buy. The Valencia film crew made a six-minute short, "No Breaks," which earned second place in a film festival in New York. It was later shown in many theaters across the country, and on Ripley's Believe It Or Not on T.V. It can still be viewed on You Tube by typing "World's Longest Sandwich (1975)" in the search bar.

In 2005, a "world's record sandwich" thirty-year reunion was staged in Taft to bring together all those who were involved in or remembered 1975's Oildorado Days, and even now people come up to me to say that they were there that day, and how much they enjoyed a literal slice of history.

Alas, our record was short-lived; it was broken only two years later. At this writing, the record is held by three teams in Beirut, Lebanon, who in May, 2011, assembled what was basically a chicken salad sandwich measuring 2,411 feet and 5 inches long. (An attempt at an even longer sandwich by a group of Iranian cooks was reputedly foiled by onlookers nibbling off one end of the sandwich before it could be measured.)

Taft is by no means out of the gigantic, gastronomic delights business. For its Oildorado Days centennial in 2010, a Domino's Pizza in Taft set the world record for the most pizzas made by a team in a 24-hour period—6,838, cranked out at the astounding rate of nearly 300 per hour.

61

TAFT'S TASTIEST GUSHER—
AN OLD-FASHIONED BANANA SPLIT

What's more enjoyable, or decadent, than an old-fashioned banana split made with a good quality ice cream finished with favorite toppings? A mega-split multiplied by 10 that serves at least eight.

Enter Gentieu's Gusher, an ice cream extravaganza of gigantic proportions, appropriately named for an area, Taft, rich in gushers of the black gold variety. The Gusher was a favorite dessert at Gentieu's West, my second restaurant. It was often ordered after sports events, school and church functions, and by friends just getting together. It came with extra long sundae spoons.

Gentieu's West had a standing challenge to anyone who could consume one Gusher within one hour. The prize: no charge and each winner's name immortalized on a brass plaque at the cash register. Eight diners loosened their belts enough to complete the chilling experience during the restaurant's five years. The victorious food warriors were always quick to point out their names when visiting the restaurant with friends. For the multitude who gave out before the bowl was empty, we had a saying, "I fought the Gusher and the Gusher won."

Gentieu's Gusher

Ingredients:

7 large scoops each of vanilla, chocolate and strawberry ice cream	Bananas, sliced
	Marshmallows
	Toasted almonds
Crushed pineapple	Chocolate and caramel syrup
Cherries	Whipped cream
Strawberries	Maraschino cherries.

Make your own ice cream party by layering 21 scoops of vanilla, chocolate and strawberry ice cream in a large glass punch bowl. Add ladles of crushed pineapple, cherries, strawberries, sliced bananas, marshmallows and toasted almonds. Squeeze on generous helpings of chocolate and caramel syrup, then finish with snowy caps of whipped cream and Maraschino cherries. Choose a few close friends and pass out the long spoons.

CHAPTER 12

THE DAY FROM HELL:
Invalid Order! Manager Required!

W e began by pin-pointing the various drain clean-outs—after touring the 6,000 or so square feet of the restaurant, we found two outside at the rear of the building, hopefully one would lead us to the blockage.

We started on the one closest to the back door, and ran an extension cord from the kitchen to power the electric snake Ben would be using to clear the blockage. He was off and running.

Returning to the kitchen, I overheard a heated exchange between one of the servers and a cook. Arguments like the one I was hearing happen all too often among staff in a high-pressure work place like a restaurant, and are tolerated to a degree. Today we had enough going on without World War Three erupting between the cooks and wait staff. My tolerance level was zero, so I jumped in to see what the shouting match was all about. A food order was missing, which the server claimed she had entered into the system, while the cook insisted that the order never made it to the kitchen printer.

The waitress station was equipped with an electronic ordering terminal on which servers entered their guests' food selections. The terminal transmitted the order to a printer in the kitchen. The printout told the cooks everything they needed to know about an order, from the desired doneness of a steak right down to hold-the-mayo requests on sandwiches. The terminal also did the math and validated the guest check. Not only did it expedite food orders conveniently and efficiently, it was a valuable tool for managing the business. The system did all this and more—when it worked. When it didn't work you needed a degree in electrical engineering to troubleshoot it.

Before heading to the waitress station I checked on Ben's progress, only to find him sitting on a pickle bucket humming and singing the Ray Charles hit, "Georgia," while he guided the snake into the clean-out at about the same tempo as the song: "Georgia, Georgia. Georgia on my mind, mmm, mmm, mmm." His rendition, complete with Ray's rocking motion, wasn't half bad, and surprisingly, Ben's singing voice was unaffected by his

DAY FROM HELL

stuttering. But under the circumstances I was more interested in the snake's progress or lack of it.

Half kidding, I asked Ben if he knew Dionne Warwick's hit, "Do You Know the Way to San Jose?" A more up-tempo tune might move things along more quickly, I reasoned, but being a Ray Charles fan through and through, Ben had limited his repertoire to just his idol's hits.

"Then you'll know this one," I chuckled, and suggested Ray's, "Hit the Road, Jack." Damn! Ben exclaimed with a slap on his knee, that's the only Ray Charles song he didn't know.

And with that, I headed back inside.

The waitress station was a scene of frenzied activity as the waitresses frantically tried to determine which orders, if any, had made it through the system to the cook line while the message, "INVALID ENTRY" intermittently flashed and blinked on the ordering terminal's screen.

Before our grand opening, the managers and their assistants were trained on the system, but I wasn't. My extra time was spent developing the menu with the kitchen staff. Gloria was new, and didn't know what to do if there was a problem like the one we were having. "Get Debbie on the horn right away!" I barked. The call went out, and the reply came back instantly: "Sorry, Len, no one answers." Where the hell could she be? She was supposed to be sick! For now, all we could do was have the waitresses give copies of their guest checks directly to the cooks, bypassing the system.

I began pressing all of its keys in an attempt to unlock the ordering terminal. Not a good idea. Not only did the machine not unlock, but it began emitting a loud beeping sound while flashing "MANAGER REQUIRED" on the screen. Now I've done it, I said to myself as the grim specter of a service technician carrying an attaché case bulging with expensive repair tools crossed my mind. The last time the ordering terminal emitted a beeping sound like this was when one of the waitresses tripped and dumped a milk shake down the back of the thing. Fixing it then required a complete overhaul of the machine with a price tag of several hundred dollars. In the present situation, if I had a pistol I would have shot the damn beeping thing.

Looking at its innards to see if something simple was causing the problem, something a chef could fix, was a saner alternative, and to avoid being electrocuted I would first have to shut off the power to the terminal. Hustling back to the main service panel and opening it, I discovered that many of the little stick-on labels that identified the individual breakers had come off and fallen to the bottom of the panel, presumably including the label for the breaker that shut off power to the order terminal. Then I remembered that the terminal required a dedicated service line, installed at great expense, with lots of head shaking and lip sucking, and its circuit breaker was in the metal enclosure behind the front panel of the waitress station. Accessing the enclosure required the removal of eight Phillips-head screws.

"Len, the people at Table 4 (the table closest to the order terminal) want to know what the beeping is. It's annoying them big time," Mildred, one of our older waitresses, informed me. "Tell them someone parked their car here and left the keys in the ignition," I snapped, and before going back to Table 4, Millie shot me the glance people give you when you've lost it, and of course I had.

My heart rate was up, my breathing rapid, and my blood seemed to race through my veins like fire. No longer was I prepared to greet anyone with love in my heart. Everything around me was turning to—well, you know what. In my mind I visualized that clip of a ski jumper on ABC's "Wide World of Sports," racing down the ski ramp and crashing near the end of his run with his skis and helmet flying wildly as he tumbled ass over teakettle down the hillside.

Banishing the image of that poor bastard from my mind, I did the only thing I could—rushed to the storeroom to gather the tools I needed to work on the order terminal.

Back at the waitress station, I crawled behind its front panel to silence the beeping terminal, tools in hand, including a dozen or so flat blade and Phillips-head screwdrivers, the crescent wrench that had seen duty in the dishwasher crisis, a crowbar, a heavy duty flashlight powered by four D cells, my variable-speed Makita electric drill with several hundred assorted drill bits, a pair of safety goggles, and of course, a hammer. One way or another, the machine's beeping was going to be silenced.

Unscrewing eight Phillips-head screws shouldn't be a problem, or so I thought. I stood the Makita case on its side and put the flashlight on top of it to shine on the screws, then chose the right screwdriver and went to work, removing one screw after another.

Half-way through, a customer spotted me and couldn't resist a jab or two. "Hey Len, what's with the beeping sound?" he asked with a smirk on his face. "Sounds like the beep you hear when you hit a jackpot in Vegas! Or is business so bad you have to jimmy the cash register?"

Ten thousand comedians out of work and this guy shows up at my place. "No jackpot, here," I grinned, "one of the girls lost a gold filling and we're tracking it down with a metal detector." A puzzled look, similar to Millie's, replaced the customer's smirk as he backed off without another word.

Four more screws to go. Screw number five had its head stripped, so the screwdriver was useless on that one. The next one came out okay, but the last two were stripped as bad as number five. The electrician who installed the enclosure hadn't given a damn if anyone ever accessed it again.

It was time to bring on the Makita. The last three screws would have to be reamed out. The drill was plugged in and ready to go when Sally, hurrying to one of her tables, tripped over the drill cord, sending the big flashlight flying and breaking the bulb. Fortunately Sally kept her balance by grabbing the Coke machine, and was none the worse for the incident.

DAY
FROM
HELL

The Invisible Revolving Door

A restaurant's entrance is the one guests use on their way to enjoying a good meal. But there's also an invisible door guests never see, the one through which employees leave for good. The restaurant industry suffers a higher turnover rate than most businesses. Let me count the ways: First, entry level jobs are usually filled with staff just passing through on their way to other career choices. They're at the restaurant mainly to earn income until better jobs open up elsewhere. Second, not everyone is cut out for a restaurant job, even though they may think they are. Restaurant work can appear glamorous in the beginning—until the staff member finds out just how demanding the work really is. At this point, he or she quickly moves on.

A restaurant's location plays an important role in its turnover rate. This was a key factor with Gentieu's West, my second restaurant, also in the small oil town of Taft. It was impossible for me to match the wages local contractors and oil companies offered. The wage gap became even wider when those companies began hiring women. We could not compete with their salaries and benefits and keep our menu pricing competitive.

Substance abuse further contributes to the high turnover, and always has. In my early days, it was not as prevalent as it is today. Back then, staff members with abuse problems were usually just fired, and the word went around they would not be good hires. Today, the industry sponsors programs to help people suffering drug, alcohol and other addictions. But these problems still cost many their jobs, even if only temporarily.

Finally, there are all the excuses and emergencies staff members conjure up that fall far short of being legitimate. It's the restaurant manager's job to sift through such claims and decide what actions to take, up to and including termination.

In my years in the business, I think I've heard just about every excuse. One that sticks in my mind was from a waitress who missed three days because she and her dog were extras in a movie, "The Best of Times" that was being filmed nearby. It starred Robin Williams and Kurt Russell in a tale about a small-town loser who gets one more shot at winning the big football game. The waitress was totally star-struck and confident Hollywood would be calling when the movie was released. Nice person, wonderful dog, but it never happened.

When hiring staff, especially managers, the screening process includes resumes, personal references, profile tests, and interviews. But in the end, hiring can still be a crap shoot. Two things I've learned is that it's all about the quality and character of the individual being considered, and that the cream always rises to the top.

With no flashlight, the stripped screws were barely visible, but just as I peered into the near darkness to position the drill, one of the servers delivered a phone message: The service technician had supplied a terminal code that should correct the problem.

I put the drill down, got up from the floor and punched in a long series of letters and numbers. Lo and behold—it worked. The beeping stopped and the screen returned to its "ENTER ORDER" mode. And just like that, the ordering system was back on line, just in time for the lunch crowd.

After instructing a busboy to put back the screws I'd removed and take the tools back to the storeroom, I headed for the kitchen. The luncheon parties had to be prepared—and Ben's progress in clearing the blockage checked on, which judging from the strains of "Georgia on My Mind" still wafting from the pickle bucket outside, was not moving along as quickly as I would have liked. On the other hand, if we ever decided to offer entertainment, I could book Ben for Friday nights.

Oh shit. Before I could get to the kitchen I encountered a very large, very determined-looking woman on her way to the still-flooded ladies' room. If she made it, the only person still dry in the restaurant would be the fire inspector safely perched on his ladder in the kitchen. I simply had to keep the lady from entering the ladies' room, and as my first line of defense, took up a blocking position in front of the door.

With the situation beginning to take on a military flavor, I flashed back to my Army days, and how the first sergeant of our outfit in Korea was always telling us how important the point man was. Being "on point" required one to be out in front to spot trouble, and warn the rest of the platoon. Rarely mentioned was the fact that the point man was often in grave danger of engaging the enemy first.

CHAPTER 13

Leonard in the Sky with Diamonds

I t's hardly a secret that alcohol and drug use, coupled with sexual promiscuity, are prevalent in the food business, challenges I suspect many other businesses also face. I'm no shrink, but let me share my take on this from the perspective of someone long on the business's front line.

The restaurant business is a high-energy industry with high-energy people. There are plenty of reasons and opportunities to indulge. Cooks might reason, at shift's end, that they've served customers all night, and now it's their turn to wind down. Or that shifts are so filled with stress, including the occasional trip to the weeds (much more on that later), that how can a drink or a joint or two be denied? The real trick is possessing enough discipline and willpower to keep a post-shift indulgence from becoming a habit that slips into addiction. The pitfalls from overdoing it are many, the most obvious being ticketed for DUI on the way home or, much worse, causing an accident in which someone is hurt or killed.

The best policy is to have one drink and not hang around too late. Too often, staff spend as much, or more time with each other as with their spouses, partners and families. We build relationships on the job by depending on each other as members of a team. Close bonds form. Combining restaurant-level stress with a lack of support or affection at home is a recipe that produces unhappy results.

Even an innocent hug can lead to less than innocent actions. Without going into detail, I will only say that sex was my drug of choice in the business. I'm not sure if my French heritage had anything to do with it, but if you could ask my father, he would say yes. However they start, affairs usually end up causing pain for everyone involved. Broken families, lost jobs, stricken finances, divorce, and sadness are but a few of the consequences, as I know from having paid the price myself.

In the early stages of my career, drug use was not prevalent. When it was present, users often flew under the radar. As the years passed, drug use became more of a problem, as it has in society in general. My experiences with most drug users on the job have been negative. As a result, I will not hire a candidate I know has a problem. Nor am I alone. These days, many restaurants require a drug test before making an offer of employment.

Pot users have disagreed with me about this, offering any number of reasons, including the "benefits" of its use. They often ask how I can make any judgments about marijuana having never tried it myself—actually I had.

My experience with marijuana began while serving with the Army in Korea in 1969. I was chef for the Commanding General of I Corps. The General's mess was staffed with a Captain, eight GIs, ten Korean nationals and myself. It was great duty considering the Vietnam conflict was raging at or near its peak. We were all happy to be stationed at I Corps. Every holiday, General Patrick Cassidy said he was proud to be serving with us out there on "Freedom's Frontier." We were also proud, and pleased, to serve in a place so well supplied with sex, booze and grass.

Two GIs from California were, in particular, no strangers to pot. On one occasion, they talked me into making marijuana brownies. The Army frowned on this type of activity, and any perpetrators were sure to be punished if caught. When the brownies came out of the oven, all gathered around with glasses of milk and beer to sample the chewy confection.

The left-over brownies were tightly sealed in Saran Wrap and stored in the rafters of the General's game room, the safest place on post to stow such contraband. A few days later, one of the guys responsible for cleaning the room discovered brownie crumbs on the pool table. They were quickly cleaned up and the remaining brownies were removed from the rafters. Rats, having discovered the stash, had left the crumbs and were reportedly seen wobbling along the upper beams of the room. Those were happy rats, we all agreed.

The brownie experience was my first exposure to the wicked weed. Years later, back in civilian life, I had another, with my first restaurant, Gentieu's Pantry, a sandwich shop and delicatessen featuring Philadelphia-style hoagies in Taft, California. The little shop employed students from the local high school, two of whom were seniors about to graduate. They thought it would be fun to get high with me, and that getting high would serve as a graduation present to them.

I liked the pair, and had not yet formed an opinion about pot smoking. At the end of the night shift, I turned the Open sign over and they got out the bong. They showed me how to place my mouth over the bong and inhale. And, unlike our former president, inhale I did. The bong turned out to be a much more serious means of getting high than the brownies. Hanging on to the bong, I kept at it with intermittent spells of coughing. The seniors were delighted. Pretty soon, we were all laughing as I prepared specialty sandwiches for everyone to eat. They told me that was a classic case of "the munchies."

My taste buds seemed more discriminating. Quality food tasted better and lesser quality food did not taste good at all, especially in the case of chocolate. The other remarkable effect was the intensity I felt just cleaning the grill top. Normally an unpleasant job, now it was fun. After a two-hour grill scrub, we called the party to a halt. I needed to lock up and drive the five blocks to my home. This was when I experienced the downside. I had to cross a two-lane road and five stop signs to make it home. But once in the car, I was hesitant to pull away from the curb. When I did, I drove half a block then pulled back to the curb. I kept watching for the police, fully expecting to be stopped any minute. The main road through town posed the biggest obstacle as I kept looking left and right, left and right, before deciding to venture across.

The trip home, usually five minutes, seemed to take an hour. At home, I still needed to get past my then-wife Kathy. That proved to be a little easier than the driving. I made it to the bedroom, and tucked myself in for a good night's sleep. The next day, the morning shift wanted to know who cleaned the grill. They thought we had installed a new one overnight. My pot-smoking partners cracked up when I described my drive home and how paranoid I was. Laughing, they told me this was a normal reaction for novice smokers.

I must admit I liked the feeling of being able to tackle as nasty a job as cleaning the grill while being both thorough and enthusiastic. Since I liked to work, I thought I might have even stumbled on to something by replacing whiskey with getting high.

Months later, I had the opportunity to expand Gentieu's Pantry by moving it to a much larger building in the West Side Shopping Center, then Taft's only shopping center. I created a new concept that combined a steak house and an ice cream parlor, and secured a bank loan to fund the venture, which I called Gentieu's West. The restaurant was a huge success right from the get go. We were smashing local sales records and quickly became the top restaurant in town. I was at the top of my game and had taken my pot-smoking cohorts along for the ride. Life was good. I was making money and felt like a big fish in a little pond.

The bankers were thrilled our loan was being paid down at an accelerated pace. I had dodged the manhole cover stage and was stashing C-notes in my wallet. My pot smoking continued but some not-so-positive effects were kicking in. One day just before the lunch rush hit, I was in the restroom next to my office getting ready to take a couple hits from my little pipe. Standing there, facing the mirror on the wall, I suddenly realized how much I had been smoking.

"Len," I said to myself, "What the hell are you doing?" Getting high had begun draining my desire to work. I was so relaxed work was becoming less important than feeling high.

I had to forcibly remind myself of the responsibilities I had to my family, my staff of fifty, the bank, even the town itself. I was at the helm of Taft's largest, most successful restaurant with sales in excess of $1 million a year. This was in the late 1970s, when the highest priced item on the menu was a $13 steak. Back then, sales of that magnitude were unprecedented in our area— the town's population was about 7,000 people. I was riding a juggernaut and taking it for granted. Gentieu's West was my most successful restaurant, and all the elements were in place to move it into a franchise phase.

Standing there, frozen in place before the mirror, a battle took place inside me. On the one hand, I could fire up the pipe and get high; on the other, I could put the pipe aside and regain control of my life.

My choice was made by a knock on the door accompanied by the shouted message that I was needed on the broiler. The lunch rush had begun and we were busy. The pipe landed in the trash can and I emptied the little baggie of buds into the toilet and flushed. That was it. I went cold turkey and never did pot again. Nor was I ever sorry. The choice I made was proof enough that pot and the restaurant business don't mix.

ENTRÉE OR ON THE SIDE— FRIED RICE A LA CHU

"I like your husband, he harrrrd worka!" Frank Chu told Midge, my wife, when they first met. I had also just recently met him. This was in the mid-1980s, shortly before Frank purchased Gentieu's West, my second eatery in Taft, and converted it to T. F. Chu's Chinese Restaurant. Chu's stood at the opposite end of the same shopping center in which I built Leonard's, my next restaurant. His became the most popular place for Chinese food and take-out, and mine became the most successful western-style restaurant in town. We became good friends.

Frank, a Chinese national, was among the most resourceful people I've ever known. He had spent eight hard years as a civilian in South Vietnam during the war, where he survived many close calls. He earned a living by gathering thousands of spent brass shell casings, which he packed and shipped back to the U.S., selling back to us as salvage the remnants of our expired firepower. Fortunately, he was able to escape Saigon before it fell in April, 1975.

Frank had been in the restaurant business prior to coming to Taft, and his expertise showed. A master at Chinese wok cookery, Frank taught me some of his favorite dishes, including his unbeatable fried rice.

Fried Rice a la Chu (serves 8)

Ingredients:

4 cups long-grain white rice, cooked

1 bunch green onions, diced

8 to 10 garlic cloves, chopped

4 carrots, julienned

1 tb. fresh ginger, minced

8 oz. thinly sliced ham, julienned

8 oz. thinly sliced turkey, julienned

4 oz. mushrooms, sliced

4 stalks celery, julienned

6 oz. bay shrimp, cooked

4 egg pancakes, cut into strips

Sesame oil

Soy sauce to taste

Rice vinegar to taste

Red chili oil to taste

As is typical of Chinese cooking, much of the work lies in the preparation; in this case, in cooking the rice, shrimp and pancakes beforehand, and in slicing and chopping the cold cuts and vegetables. Once everything has been gathered and readied, heat a wok or a heavy pan over a fire until very hot, add the sesame oil, then add the green onions, garlic, carrots, ginger, ham, turkey, mushrooms, celery, and shrimp.

Stir fry all the ingredients together for just a few minutes. Add the rice and stir fry a couple more minutes. Remove the food from the fire, moisten with a little soy sauce and rice vinegar and, sparingly, the red chili oil. Serve with the sliced egg pancakes and a few chopped green onions on top. It makes a wonderful side dish and includes enough protein to also work as a main course for lunch or dinner.

CHAPTER 14

THE DAY FROM HELL:
One Small Piece of Romaine

With my legs spread and feet planted firmly, hands raised like a Ninja warrior's, I prepared to greet the gal with the bad news about the restroom closure. I was not going to risk her ignoring the out-of-order sign hastily put up by Albert. (He had misspelled "order," so the sign read, "Out of Odor," but that wasn't exactly true either.)

The lady was closing fast and my body tensed up as she stopped directly in front of me. I spoke first with a polite, "Hello."

"I have to go to the bathroom," she answered.

"I'm so sorry, the restrooms are temporarily out of order," I informed her.

"Why?" A reasonable question, and while trying to think of an answer I remained calm except for the twitching in my right eye that was beginning to tear up, as if I were weeping. "The plumber is here and addressing the problem," I told the lady.

"I have to go now. I can't wait for the plumber!" was her answer.

"I understand, I'm sorry for the inconvenience."

"I'll just take my business elsewhere!" the lady fumed and stomped out. What business was that? I mused.

I could understand the lady's anger, but couldn't help feeling I had just won a battle. I began to hum the theme from the "Bridge on the River Kwai." Just hearing it motivated me again and reminded me of the camp commandant telling his prisoners, "You must be happy in your work!" as they assembled to receive their harsh duty assignments. I decided I was going to be happy in my work and have love in my heart, even if it killed me.

I started for the kitchen again. The couple at Table 20 had a question about the pickled tongue appetizer (what was it?) and waved for me to join them. I greeted them with my customary "what can I do for you?" and just as they began to speak, out of the corner of my eye I glimpsed the heavy-set woman passing the salad bar as she was leaving the restaurant in

DAY FROM HELL

search of a restroom. In her path lay a large, crisp leaf of romaine lettuce. It could have fallen on the tiled floor from the salad cart when the prep cook brought the salads out from the kitchen, or been dropped there by a careless diner.

I quickly calculated that with two more steps, the lady's right foot would land squarely on the leaf. I wanted to shout out a warning, but couldn't. My heart sank, my mind raced, my lungs took in a breath as if it were their last. But for my brain, my body was in a state of total paralysis. Adding to the potential for a calamity, Domingo, the busboy, was passing behind the lady carrying a full tray of dirty dishes, unaware that if the lady should tumble, he would be flattened like a pancake.

My demeanor must have been puzzling to the diners at Table 20. They were still valiantly trying to talk to me but my eyes were riveted on the woman and the lettuce leaf. My eye started twitching again, and compounding my plight, I was practically succumbing to nature's call myself. All the coffee I had been gulping down that morning was having its effect, as was the catastrophe I was about to witness, and I stood there with my legs crossed, trying mightily to avoid an accident and considering the distinct possibility that the woman I had my eyes on was going to be my new business partner, courtesy of the lettuce leaf and our legal system.

The lady's foot hit the romaine leaf dead center, and upon being crushed, the leaf acted as if it were oil between the tile and the woman's shoe, causing her right leg to fly forward and upward. With her right leg extended skyward, all of the lady's weight shifted to her left leg. Her extended arms began flailing in a circular, windmilling motion that helped keep her upright, reminding me of someone trying to stay balanced while pedaling in a log-rolling contest.

I prayed for a miracle while Domingo, who at last had seen what was going down, sped out of harm's way at Mach One speed. In his hasty retreat, his foot caught the base of the salad bar. Stumbling, he managed to stay upright, but half the contents of his tray crashed to the floor with the sound of a bomb going off.

All eyes turned in the direction of the crash and caught the balancing act in progress in front of the salad bar. With Domingo now out of the way, my view was unobstructed, making me the best possible eyewitness for the insurance adjuster.

Yet still the lady stood, perfectly balanced on her left leg in a scene of surreal beauty unfolding as if it were a slow motion ballet. But the strain on the lady's left leg proved to be too much, and the leg began to buckle. This was going to be it, the biggest lawsuit in Taft's history, I grimaced, but recognizing that I was captain of this ship, it was my duty to go down with it.

I rushed toward the lady, lacking any training from chef's school as to what to do in this kind of emergency, and as I raced past Table 4 I overheard the customer sitting there softly whisper, "Holy shit." Eight-year old Jimmy Bradford sitting at the next table with his parents, had a

different take on the spectacle. "Cool!" he exclaimed, and took another bite of his corn dog.

As I slid through the debris from Domingo's dumped tray, the lady's right leg miraculously returned to solid ground. With both feet now firmly planted on the floor, her arms began windmilling in reverse, then slowly came to rest at her sides. The room suddenly burst into applause. Everyone, believe me, was thankful for the lady's safe landing, and after checking to make sure she was okay, I happily escorted her to the door while the help cleaned up the shattered dishware.

Meanwhile, I'd understandably experienced some leakage from the incident. My slacks had taken a hit, but fortunately their dark color concealed my accident. Even after the panic subsided I still had to go, and badly, restroom out of order or not, and began hustling over to the men's room like a penguin shuffling across the Antarctic ice, only faster.

Before I could get to the men's room I had to make my way through a dining room filled with customers who wanted to re-live the remarkable performance we had just witnessed or engage in other chit chat. A problem, considering my condition.

"Hey Len, c'mon over!" bellowed Joe, a regular ensconced with his buds in Booth 8.

You don't have to go, I told myself before stopping at Joe's booth. You're a camel. You can hold it. Keep those legs tight.

With my head bobbing and my eyelid twitching while I muttered this self-talk under my breath, I could easily have been mistaken for someone suffering from Tourette's syndrome. If I suddenly started cursing uncontrollably, there would be no doubt.

"Len, did you watch the game this weekend?," Joe asked. "Did you see that spectacular shot at the last second that won it?" he grinned, feeling the need to share the thrill of victory with anyone who would listen.

As a working chef and owner, my weekends are invariably consumed by 17-hour work days, leaving little time for watching sports on TV. That said, on a normal day I would have shared Joe's enthusiasm, but today was anything but normal and my mind (and body) were otherwise occupied, to put it mildly.

I showed an obligatory interest in what Joe was saying, then gracefully excused myself and hurried to the out-of-order restroom where I was greeted by the welcome sight of a trio of shiny white urinals with no one standing before them.

After taking care of business and a thorough hand wash, I headed back to the office to strip off my dress slacks and Jockey shorts and put on my chef pants, which I wore commando-style the rest of the day.

Interestingly, the traditional chef's uniform of black-and-white checked pants and white jacket were devised by Marie-Antoine Carême, a 19th-century French chef considered to be one of the world's first "celebrity" chefs. A white, double-breasted jacket, made of cotton with rope buttons, is the top half of Carême's design. The white material denotes cleanliness,

DAY FROM HELL

and with the double-breasted feature, a clean jacket front can be folded over to hide one stained from kitchen spills. Rope buttons were used to withstand repeated washings, and the checkered pattern of the pants served to camouflage stains. The "toque," the familiar tall white hat chefs wear, was also standardized by Carême, and often indicated rank within the kitchen. The toque's hundred folds are said to represent the many ways a chef knows how to cook an egg. To this day, Carême's outfit is the most common uniform of any type worn in the western world. Modern chefs, however, have modified the traditional design to express their personal styles, adding colors and other design changes.

Dressed and dry, it was back to the kitchen where I found the fire inspector waiting —and the flood water gone. Ben must have succeeded in clearing the blockage. All that remained to be done was mop the kitchen and restroom floors with a disinfectant, followed by a second mopping with bleach and hot water, then a deep cleaning later that night after the restaurant closed.

After signing the fire inspector's paperwork I went outside to congratulate Ben of Benjamin's plumbing. He was pulling the snake out of the clean-out and holding a running water hose to flush out the drain, which had been partially blocked by tree roots and other debris. A piece of dish towel at the end of Ben's snake told the rest of the story. The remnant was from the same towel that had blocked the dishwasher's pump impeller earlier that morning. It had worked its way down the main drain line, completing the blockage, and my first impulse was to get my hands on the S.O.B. who caused the problem. So much for love in my heart.

Relieved to have the blockage cleared, I went back to the office. By late morning I usually switched from coffee to ice cold Cokes. Today was no exception. The Cokes provided an instant kick, and there were always Hershey bars to fall back on. Not very nutritious, but a snack that jump started the rest of the day. That's typical of how meals are taken by staff— when we eat is determined by the restaurant's business. When it's busy, staff just keeps on truckin', consuming food on the fly.

CHAPTER 15

The Show Must Go On

In 1982, about nine weeks into developing the space for Leonard's, and having already spent over $200,000, our progress had slowed to a snail's pace. The completion date had been extended several times and was still in doubt. I was concentrating on dealing with challenges I could handle—riding herd on a crew of plumbers, carpenters, electricians and the like. Meanwhile, the cash flow was all outgoing, a situation we desperately needed to reverse. It was vital to have some sense of when the work would be complete.

Remodeling a building—in this case, a space in a shopping center—for a restaurant start-up is a monumental, even overwhelming job. At the beginning, it's all excitement and anticipation. As the project progresses and the hard work sets in, most of the excitement and anticipation diminishes. There are a myriad of agencies, suppliers, contractors, workers, accountants and bankers that must be dealt with. It's a difficult process that inevitably runs over any budget established at the start. I have been through five start-ups of my own, and each was more expensive and difficult than the one before.

On this job, every day was filled with excuses. One Friday, I was steadying a 12-foot section of dry wall while the carpenter was securing it to the stud wall that separated the kitchen from the dining room. The plumber came by to tell me he would be taking the rest of the day off. The news shot through my brain like a thunderbolt.

The problem was the restroom, which still wasn't functional. A working restroom had been promised early into the job, so there would be no need to rent a Port-a-Potty to put in the parking lot adjacent to the restaurant.

4-Daily Midway Driller, Taft, Ca., Nov. 18, 1982

Restaurant to feature 1800's theme

Construction is underway for Leonard's, a new restaurant to be located in the former Boat Shop building at 1015 Fourth St. Owner Leonard Gentieu says the restaurant theme will depict a period of the late 1800's.

"There will be four dining areas, each with unique and distinctive atmosphere, furnished with oak wood tables, old-fashioned chairs and ceiling fans, complimented by decorative lighting of the same period, Gentieu said.

An old-fashioned oakwood hearth will be the focal point in the kitchen, he said.

"A great deal of time and expense went into its construction."

"Many of the featured menu items will be broiled over oakwood embers, resulting in a delicious taste and flavor unobtainable with conventional gas broiling," he said.

The restaurant layout is being handled by Design Restaurant Supply in Oakland.

"We are presently in the construction phase of the project, which should last approximately seven weeks," Gentieu said.

"We anxiously await the conclusion of the construction, taking off our hard hats and putting on our chef hats, returning to the kitchen to prepare foods we hope you will enjoy.

"We look forward to serving all our friends and customers and we thank you for your patience."

Other recent remodeling projects in the shopping center had done just that only to be victimized by vandals pushing the johns over at night. I wasn't about to risk that kind of harassment.

The other stores in the center did not want us coming in to use their facilities. The workers went to a nearby gas station. I lived a couple blocks away, and got in my truck and drove home when nature called. All this added to the delay in getting the job done. Yet still no restroom.

We had already jack-hammered a 30-foot trench in the cement floor to run lines to the main sewer hook-up under the parking lot. I had spent a full back-breaking day on the jack hammer myself. The tile work was done, a beeswax ring had been set in the floor, and a water-line nipple had been capped and stood ready to hook up. A nice new toilet was even sitting in a box waiting to be uncrated. There was no reason the toilet could not have been installed immediately, and in service for all of us to use on the weekend.

"Can you handle the rest of this dry wall sheet?" I asked the carpenter. "I have to have a little talk with the plumber."

"Got you covered, Len," the carpenter answered.

"Yo, Bob, it's just 11:30," I advised the plumber. "Are you sick? Why are you taking off so early?"

"It's my birthday," Bob quickly answered, and announced that his company allowed its employees to work half a day on their birthdays.

"Wow, how cool is that," I said, thinking who the hell did Bob think he was—Lincoln, Washington, Martin Luther King? "So, it's like a paid holiday?" I added.

"You bet!" he replied.

"Tell me, did you get the toilet set this morning?"

"Didn't get 'er done today, but will have it finished for sure, first thing Monday morning," Bob said.

I felt like tearing his head off. Don't lose your temper, I told myself, consider Bob's position. It's his birthday. Well, BFD! How could I get him to hook up the fucking toilet?

"Bob, grab a Coke, I want to run something by you I think you'll find interesting." I said, taking a seat with him. "Let's say you hire me to cater your daughter's wedding," I began. "Of course, we'll spend a lot of time well in advance of the wedding date discussing all the details with your wife, daughter and in-laws. There'll be the menu, the service, the wine selection, staffing, clean-up, etc. Are we good so far?"

Bob nodded his head in agreement.

"It's going to be spectacular, an event you'll be proud of," I said. "Now, let's say all the invitations have been mailed with an almost 100 percent response. Everyone can't wait to come. You have a wonderful family, and I'm stoked because you chose us to do the job. Then on the eve of the great day, I call with bad news. Bob, I'm sorry to report the prime ribs for the main course weren't delivered today and won't be available until Monday. On top of this, two servers forgot to tell me your daughter's wedding date just happened to be the same as their wedding anniversaries. To do our part to make this the joyous occasion it should be, we give our workers their anniversaries off, which I'm sure you can appreciate. Also, my assistant cook is celebrating his son's sixth birthday with a party and has to be there to organize the birthday games. And so I say to you, darn, these things come up from time to time. Tell you what, we'll have everything worked out by Monday. You can count on it. Just call your guests and inform them of the rescheduling. What do you think, Bob? Would that be a stressful weekend?"

"Hell, yes!"

"Now, do you think I would let you down and do that to you or find some way to make your daughter's wedding happen?"

"Len, knowing you, you would make it happen."

"Bob, I think you're now ready to solve our problem." Bob, sorry to say, is a little slow. "Let me spell it out for you—I feel the same way about my crapper as you feel about your daughter's wedding. Somehow, some way, we're going to make it happen! Could you strap on the tool belt and install my toilet before you head for your birthday festivities?"

"Sure, Len, consider it done."

Mission accomplished. I just love this exercise. It works every time without having to pitch a fit, something I used to do in my early days with very little success.

THE MONEY MATRIX

Ever wonder why a $12 store-bought bottle of wine lists for $32 at your local eatery? Did the words "What a rip-off" flash through your mind? What you may not know is the average profit in an independent, full-service restaurant runs between four and twelve percent. For example, a dinner party for six with a total check of $250 yields for most full-service restaurants a profit between $15 and $30, and they wash all the dishes when you've finished the meal.

Of course, there are exceptions and owners enjoy some perks that take the place of monetary compensation. But perks only go so far. The bottom line is a restaurant has to make money and produce a cash flow to pay its bills. And if perks become excessive, the bills don't get paid.

Most restaurants work on carpaccio-thin margins, and even these numbers can be difficult to achieve. The restaurant operator has to constantly stay on top of food costs and operating percentages. The customer, of course, is the most important component in a restaurant's profitability equation. Without customer patronage, there's no way to be profitable. Thus, customer volume is also essential, and attracting new and repeat customers is crucial to making the numbers work.

Restaurants usually categorize their expenditures by converting dollars amounts to percentages based on the restaurant's sales. When sales go up, percentages improve if the restaurateur is running the business efficiently. You, the customer are responsible for the sales through your visits. Typically, restaurants work with a 60 to 70 percent gross profit after deducting the cost of goods sold (C.O.G.S.). The C.O.G.S. is broken out for food and, in the case of a bar, liquor. The gross profit (G.P.) has to also cover all the other expenses incurred.

The C.O.G.S. for a full-service restaurant should range between 30 and 36 percent. Steakhouses and fine dining operations usually run the percentage a few points higher. The challenges involved in maintaining consistent C.O.G.S. percentages are many and varied. Market conditions are not always predictable, with food prices regularly fluctuating, especially on produce and meats. This can adversely affect the C.O.G.S. and the profit. Usually, the restaurateur has to absorb any increased costs until he or she is forced to raise menu prices. Raising prices is an agonizing decision that can cause customer counts to go down—even if they don't, the fear they will is always present. Spoilage and theft also erode the profit percentage and, combined with changing prices, can shrink the bottom line by a full percentage point.

Restaurant operators can identify problems and trends that affect business by carefully watching their Profit and Loss Statements. But most operators lack the luxury of an in-house financial person, making cost-watching another duty added to everything else for which they are responsible. Even though the information on a P & L form is after the fact, it's one of a restaurant's most valuable tools. Some operations create mini-P & Ls, tracking their businesses on a weekly or even daily basis. Closely monitoring this information gives operators a chance to make adjustments quickly.

After C.O.G.S., labor is the biggest expense, and it can eat up another 30 to 40 cents of an operator's dollar. In addition to the labor itself, are the allied costs of payroll taxes, worker's comp insurance, and any employee benefits. The greatest portion of the labor cost is a fixed expense. During slow times, a skeleton crew can be used to reduce labor costs, even to the extent of using managers to take on jobs like cooking, bartending and waiting tables. But great care has to be taken to avoid lowering standards. Scheduling everything becomes an intricate balancing act. Spending more than 70 cents out of a restaurant's dollar on food and labor makes it increasingly difficult to achieve any level of profit.

The remaining 30 cents (30 percent) get gobbled up by costs that leave little room for tweaking. They include, but are not limited to, the rent or mortgage for the space, utilities, insurance, advertising, equipment leases, legal expenses, taxes not related to payroll, common area charges, equipment replacement, building maintenance, waste removal, accounting, management, outside services such as pest control, janitorial fees, hood and fire inspections, and more.

The list can go on and on! Little wonder, by the time all expenses are met, the owner considers the business a success if he or she's still holding onto four to twelve cents out of every dollar. The key to succeeding is sales volume. If a restaurant can increase the number of its customers, the percentages it spends in each category should go down. Conversely, when customer volume goes down, percentages go up, until the levels are no longer sustainable.

It's worth mentioning that menu sales, discount promotions, daily specials, holiday sales, banquets and outside catering are also very important considerations in measuring the pulse of a business and increasing its profit potential.

Sad to say, speaking as an independent restaurateur, chain or franchise operations usually perform much better than independents. Most have so refined their business models that they know how successful a new unit will be before they open it. They miss on occasion, but rarely. The economies of scale they realize as a result of the large number of customers going through their doors enable them to operate more efficiently. This is their biggest advantage. But they also ruthlessly control expenses, and track their numbers, including percentages, daily, even hourly. They also use the numbers to hold managers accountable by measuring performance against them. A chain manager lives or dies by the percentages. When they're missed, termination is around the corner.

The next time you're enjoying a meal with friends at a favorite restaurant and the bill is presented, consider the percentages outlined above and do the math. You may be surprised at how reasonable the cost will then seem.

CHAPTER 16

THE DAY FROM HELL:
Floods, Flags and Forks

With my blood sugar skyrocketing, I was ready to take on the stuck cash drawer. Distracted by everything else, I had, of course, forgotten to call the locksmith. Piss on the key. Let's go with brute force. This was one job my trusty sidekick would be the right tool for, so I went into the storeroom and got the hammer and a big-ass screwdriver. Returning to the cashier's stand, I jammed the screwdriver between the lock and the drawer face and pounded the shit out of it. Voila—problem solved!

I rewarded myself with another Coke, and turned to the set-ups for the parties booked for the two banquet rooms. We were short on forks, I learned from the bus boy doing the set-up in the West Side Room. "Okay, check the storeroom and get a couple dozen for Albert to wash," I instructed him.

Glassware and silverware are always at a premium due to breakage and loss. We kept a backup supply to account for this, and used a clipboard in the storeroom to sign out new items placed in service. The clipboard also helped us keep an eye on inventory. Like the other controls we had, it worked fine when followed, but wasn't worth a damn if items were not checked off and signed for when they were taken. Today, of course, there were no extra forks. Sometimes it's the little things that get you.

Meanwhile, the Gaslight Room was being set up for the Kiwanis Club luncheon. A head table for eight, to be presided over by the visiting dignitary, would have to be set up, and various banners and other trappings hung for display on the back wall of the banquet room.

The fork shortage also cropped up in the Gaslight Room. It was up to the day managers to solve this kind of problem, but Gloria was too busy and Debbie was out, and so it fell to me. Pretty soon I was giving orders left and right. First: Skip the salad forks, everyone gets a single fork. Second: be ready to serve within the hour. Third: check with me before serving the salads.

DAY FROM HELL

The cook line had regained momentum, now that the flooding had stopped. Albert had mopped up the water, and with the order terminal fixed, the cooks' printer was working again, eliminating the tension between the cooks and wait staff.

Things seemed to be returning to normal. The chicken breasts had arrived, and the first cook had prepared a delicious Chicken Marsala. Earlier, I had managed to talk the representative of the Kiwanis Club into a nice stir fry for their party, a dish that was easy to prepare from what was on hand in the walk-in. It also saved us from having to use the chicken reserved for the baby shower.

I had Margie, the first cook, prepare a large batch of rice pilaf, enough for both parties, while I prepared the stir fry. This is where my skill and speed showed their worth. I quickly went to work on the *mise en place*.

"*Mise en place*," French for "everything in place," refers to everything a cook will need to prepare the menu items that can be ordered during his or her shift. It's something every chef learns early on. "Make ready your station," was the rallying cry in chef's school and in the first restaurant I worked in. "*Mise en place! Mise en place!*"

In those days one never questioned the chef. I have witnessed chefs throwing pots, pans, dishes, fully-plated food, even knives across their kitchens, accompanied by the foulest of curses. Sad as I am to admit it, I have been guilty of this out-of-control behavior, too. It was part of the culture then. Thankfully it's rarely tolerated today, making the kitchen a much better work place.

The food prep for the two luncheons was coming together nicely, but serving the parties in addition to the lunch crowd would push our short-handed wait staff to its limit.

I instructed Eddie, normally our breakfast cook, to plate-up 75 salads, rack them, and wheel them into the walk-in, ready for service, then tray-up the dinner rolls for heating in the oven. Our approach to party catering, especially in-house, is to complete the final cooking as close to the service time as possible. Preparing food in advance then letting it sit in warmers ahead of service never improves the food's quality. Waiting till the last minute for final cooking is similar to what we do on the cook line when a guest orders off the menu. We prepare the dish "*a la minute*," in an instant, insuring that the guest receives a quality dish.

The cook's job is to prepare the food as ordered, when ordered. It is sent out on a heated plate under a food warmer on the pick-up shelf while the cook calls out the words "pick-up, pick-up," often accompanied by a tap on a bell. Good line cooks want their orders to move as quickly as possible. If a dish sits too long under the heating elements, it can develop a thin, opaque layer on top, especially if it's covered by a sauce. This is a tell-tale sign the cooks or wait staff are not paying enough attention to serving the food as soon as it's ready.

It still drives me crazy to see that, especially because attention to detail is what keeps customers coming back, and repeat business is good business, considering how costly it is to attract new customers. And because the pick-up counter is the fault line where friction between the cooks and wait staff occurs, picking up orders promptly keeps things moving smoothly, and clears the pick-up station for the next orders going out.

We were about ten minutes away from beginning service for our two luncheon parties. Since timing would be critical, I planned to stagger the service of the salad courses to allow more time between serving the two main courses, alleviating some of the pressure on the wait staff.

Word came from the Gaslight Room that the flag stand the Kiwanis Club used in its meetings was missing. Nancy, one of our top servers, was passing through the kitchen, and I asked her if she could find out what happened to it.

"Len, the hostess just sat three tables in my section. I'm sorry but I can't spare the time," she answered, and she was right about that. None of the other waitresses could either. I'll have to take this one, I said to myself, and headed for the Gaslight Room.

"Hey, what's this I'm hearing about a missing flag stand?" I asked Charlie, a Kiwanis Club member I knew.

"The busboy can't find the damn thing and we need it for the table our exalted ruler from out of town will be sitting at. It's a must have," was Charlie's answer. The flag stand was about three feet long, shaped like an inverted crescent, and drilled full of holes that held the flags of the various countries the Kiwanis Club had established chapters in, and was the centerpiece of their meetings.

"Charlie, I thought you guys took that thing home after your meetings and brought it back for the next one."

"I know. I usually bring it, but must have left it here after our last meeting." Charlie's goof had suddenly become my problem. Of all days for this to happen, why today? I bend over backward to accommodate the group, and they throw me a curve ball!

"I'll have one of my people look for it," I told Charlie.

"I hope you find it," he answered glumly. "Without the flags, our chapter will really look bad in front of the top guy."

You would think from the worried look on Charlie's face that we had lost the Ark of the Covenant. Surely the flag stand's absence would not keep the Kiwanis people from eating lunch. But I could sympathize with Charlie's plight. This was supposed to be his moment in the sun, and it looked like he was going to blow it.

"Albert!" I shouted, "check the storeroom and any other place you can think of and see if you can find the flag stand the Kiwanis people set up at their meetings."

"Len, I'm trying to keep up with the silverware washing," he answered. "The waitresses are screaming for forks so they can finish their set-ups."

"Albert, do you think you're telling me something I don't already know? Okay, stay with the silverware." The Kiwanis people would just have to eat unaccompanied by the flags of the world.

DAY FROM HELL

Suddenly, the lunch hour was in full swing. The kitchen printer was spitting out orders as fast as the cooks could tear them off and in the middle of all this activity a server working the Kiwanis Club party burst into the kitchen with the news that the missing flag stand had been found.

"Well, hallelujah. Where the hell was it?" I asked.

"Charlie found it in the trunk of his car. When he came in from the parking lot all excited and laughing he asked me to pass the good news along with his apology."

"And just what was that, pray tell?"

"'My bad, my bad.'"

My good, my good, I thought. At least now they can eat. I asked the server if she was ready for the salads.

"The drinks have been served and we're all set. I'll pull the rolls and get them out first."

"Great. Albert, bring the rack of salads from the walk-in and dress forty of them."

"What about the silverware?"

"Get the salads now!" This was no time for Albert to be problem solving. He was in his comfort zone with the silverware washing, and unaware that he was about to become part of our stretching exercise.

"Margie, I'll have Albert run your salads for the West Side Room. Will you be ready to fire their main course in about 15 minutes?"

"Len, I don't think I should leave the line. Orders are piling up and we just got a large take-out order from one of the oil companies. They're in a hurry, and want to pick up in 20 minutes. They've ordered all our specialty sandwiches, including six large Capacola Subs."

"Good call, stay put."

CHAPTER 17

Apocalypse Leonard's

Four years into the operation of Leonard's, Midge and I experienced our first real burn out. Leonard's was my third and largest restaurant in Taft, after Gentieu's Pantry and Gentieu's West. Paradoxically, it was my most successful and most disastrous restaurant experience—the best of times and the worst of times.

Restaurant ventures rank near the top of the list of tough, risky businesses to own and operate. They involve innumerable moving parts, long working hours, high stress levels, razor-thin margins, and multiple revolving doors through which people at all levels come, go, and sometimes return. Workers at every stratum—from owners, chefs and managers, to cooks and the wait staff—are susceptible to burn out. Add the gasoline of family discord and con artists' promises and the sky's the limit as to what can go wrong.

And in our case, it did.

Leonard's was structured as a partnership between Midge and myself, with my older brother, Paul, and his wife, Cindy, as minority owners. Our partnership, like so many, started happily, with everyone excited and working well together. I was the General Manager, Midge served as the Day Manager, Paul was in charge of purchasing and cutting meat, and Cindy was the Night Manager. Everything seemed simple and logical.

Not long after opening, Paul began a cross-country trucking business, leaving Cindy to hold the fort during his frequent absences. I soon took over the butchering along with providing supervision for the cooking staff on the night shift. Most of my days began at 7 a.m., and finished between 9 and 10 p.m.—longer on weekends. The hours were grueling, but I was still young.

With Paul gone much of the time, Cindy began losing interest in the restaurant. After several months, operations began to unravel. The first warning sign was the deteriorating attitude of the night crew, fueled by Cindy's increasing negativity. Soon, an unhealthy rivalry developed between the night and the day crews. This is actually not unusual—a little friendly competition, kept in check, can improve morale. But this rivalry was becoming a problem. As GM, it was my responsibility to solve it.

I explained to Cindy that it was not good to pit the day and night crews against each other, and that this attitude was affecting the operation. I suggested she change places with Midge for a month to better understand the day shift. She was reluctant, and only agreed to appear supportive of our efforts. Her words proved hollow; nothing changed.

Before our first year had ended, it became clear we harbored strong differences about leadership and management styles. We were not getting along as partners and felt it would be in everyone's best interest to end it. Paul and Cindy did not like California and were anxious to return to Delaware, so Midge and I agreed to buy them out.

Our accountant told us the business was too young and carrying too much debt to show much value. He suggested we pay Paul and Cindy their initial investment plus 10 percent interest. The idea did not fly with them. I finally asked the dollar amount they wanted. After some heated negotiations, we agreed on an offer they were willing to accept, one I thought was very generous. In less than a year, they would more than double their original investment. I would have been more than happy to take the offer had our situations been reversed. (I later learned that the rest of the family back East believed I was the bad guy, having only heard one side of the story.)

For me, it was back to the bank to secure additional funds for the buyout. But as we were already heavily in debt with our initial loan, the bank was reluctant to advance more just because I couldn't make my partnership work.

Of course, to an entrepreneur, "no" is merely a suggestion. First, I informed the bank I was the most qualified person to continue on with Leonard's operation. Second, I said that if they reviewed my loan payment history, it would show that I had paid off all previous loans on time. My track record was good and everyone I dealt with there knew I always paid my bills on time.

It is universally known that when you don't need a bank's money, it will proffer all kinds of loans you don't need, but when you do need the money, it will be like pulling hens' teeth to get it. Luckily, this bank proved to be an exception. They decided to fund the buyout, counting on my ability to keep Leonard's solvent, so that its much larger loan would be paid off in the future. The bank wrote the buyout check and Paul and Cindy were off to Delaware.

A week passed and the bank called me in for a meeting. I wondered if it might have to do with Charlie Reid, the co-signer on our initial loan. Charlie was a local electrical contractor who had volunteered to help Midge and I get the loan approved. At the bank, I was informed Charlie was pulling his signature—suddenly, the note was due and payable, along with the subsequent loan for the partnership buyout.

This was devastating news. I knew that the partnership's break-up had everything to do with Charlie's decision. After some investigation, I learned many untruths had been told to Charlie about Midge and myself, but his decision was made—and final.

I asked the loan officer why we couldn't go forward without Charlie's signature. We were current with our payments and Leonard's was becoming more profitable. He said his hands were tied because there was no longer enough equity in the restaurant to support the loan without a co-signer. He was sorry, but bank policy was dictated from the home office.

He suggested I immediately begin looking for new funds as the home office would be turning up the heat to get the loans paid off. The bank giveth and the bank taketh, after first letting me spendeth; I was really pissed.

"What's the bank going to do?" I replied in my best sotto voce version of a shout, "send a team over in chef coats to take my place? If so," I ranted, "I will pack up my knives and they can have it!" Then I stormed out of the bank, even though I knew deep down that no one ever won an argument by leaving the room.

As a result of the buyout, Midge and I were already more deeply indebted than ever. Now we were back at square one on the loan question, and the morale of Leonard's staff was continuing to decline. The episode took its toll not only on us but the restaurant as well. We needed to get back to the business of running it and, with the increased debt, the more efficiently the better.

Midge and I jumped back in, working the extra hours needed to cover all the shifts. It was an enormous strain that stretched us to the limits, physically and mentally. Yet tired as we were, we slowly made progress and grew the business.

Donning coat and tie, I hit the streets searching for a new loan, something I dreaded as I vividly remembered being rejected by sixteen banks before Charlie stepped up as co-signer. I was not optimistic, but a couple weeks into the process I thought I would check with a new local bank.

I sat down with Margo, the loan officer, and began my tale of woe. Since Taft was a small town, Margo was well aware of the restaurant and others I had owned. She even brought up the Guinness record-breaking sandwich made years earlier, when I owned Gentieu's Pantry. We discussed numbers for close to an hour, then she left to speak with Gene Smith, the bank's president. After a few minutes, she returned to tell me they would do the deal and the money would be available by the end of the week.

I felt a presence heavy and malign as an incubus lift from my shoulders. I offered Margo my tax returns, profit and loss statements, personal financial statements, all the stuff loan applications usually require. She said they could get that information later and that they were granting the loan based

89

more on my years of local business experience. This was unbelievingly refreshing.

I gleefully returned to my old bank and requesting the precise amount of my loans, which I would be paying off by the end of the week. I also took the opportunity to close my personal, business and savings accounts—they would be moved to Taft National Bank along with the more than $1 million in yearly deposits from Leonard's. Taft National was placing a big bet I would be successful. I appreciated the support and the faith they had in me.

I was also more determined than ever to make Leonard's not only the best restaurant in town but the most profitable. But that was not entirely in my control, despite the 90-hour weeks Midge and I were enduring. Taft's economy depended on the oil industry and, early in 1987, the oil market crashed in what came to be known as "the third oil shock." Wells were shut, crews laid off, and "West Texas Crude" fell to $10 a barrel. Oil in our area sold at under $10. In October, the stock market took a beating, which didn't help. With people being laid off in large numbers, fewer of them could afford to eat out.

Our business plunged by a third almost overnight, and our corporate business with oilfield contractors and petroleum corporations promised to slow as well. Everyone thought the crisis would be short lived. So did we. We maintained our staff of over 50 with just a cutback in hours.

After two months struggling to make payroll, with our savings exhausted, we had no choice but to lay off half the crew in a desperate effort to survive the downturn. Our profits vanished and we began selling off other assets like cars and furniture and emptying out what retirement funds we had. Anything not nailed down went on the auction block.

By summer's end Midge and I were exhausted and hanging on by a thread financially. Having weathered everything up to then, I finally hit the wall. Going in each day became a ritual of just grinding out the work. I had lost the joy of cooking. Given the heavy debt and with our future receipts questionable, the only relief I could see for us was to sell the restaurant before we both ended up in the hospital. I told Midge we needed to do this while the numbers were still good enough to attract a buyer. But months went by without so much as a nibble. We were barely managing to pay the bills.

It was the lowest point in my career. I was drinking heavily just to get through each day. Nights spent cooking on the broiler were usually interrupted by severe chest pains that would take me to my knees. The other cooks would often send me to the office to rest while they took care of the cook line. It was a scary time and I seriously questioned—for the first time in my life—how long I could keep going at this pace.

One afternoon, the cashier told me a gentleman named Raul wanted to speak with me. I introduced myself, and we sat down to talk. Raul asked if the restaurant might be for sale. I could scarcely believe it. Was the answer to our prayers sitting there before me? It might be, I replied, as Midge and I were ready to move on to other things.

I realized Raul was very religious when he told me God had something for him in Taft. He clasped a Bible in one hand and a church hymnal in the other. Who was I to question God? I thought. Frankly, I was so far down the tubes, I didn't care if he'd been sent by God or Smokey the Bear. We scheduled a meeting at which Midge and I would meet his wife.

A week later we learned more about their background. They were both deeply involved in a large church with a congregation of over 4,000, in Orange County. His wife was in charge of the ladies' ministries and he was the church treasurer. They had been led to Taft, they said, and the possible ownership of Leonard's. Raul claimed many years of restaurant management experience, with his most recent a large restaurant in the South Coast Plaza in Costa Mesa. Unlike Midge, Raul's wife worked outside the restaurant business.

I made several phone calls to verify their claims and asked for references, most of which yielded lukewarm responses offering no specifics, good or bad. This is a tactic used all the time when a candidate does not deserve a good recommendation, and a red flag to which I should and would have paid attention, had I not been so desperate.

We met again to discuss the selling price and terms, and reached an agreement. The next step was for them to secure funding. Weeks passed before we met to review their progress or lack thereof, as it turned out.

The banks were unwilling to make Raul a loan, which was not surprising considering all I had gone through for financing. I asked Taft National if they could assume my existing loan and was quickly turned down. I offered to carry a note if they could come up with at least 10 percent down on the purchase price. Finally, one bank showed interest and promised an answer in a few days, but the answer was no. I phoned the banker to ask why and was told something they were not able to discuss with me had come up in the application process. Red flag number two!

We decided to draw up a management contract with an option for the couple to purchase Leonard's by making monthly payments generated by the restaurant's receipts, effectively securing the sales price with my own asset. The only skin Raul would have in the game would be his labor, a type of deal not to be found in any business manuals.

We set a takeover date and introduced the couple to the staff. I called all our suppliers to tell them we were leaving the business and to transfer our accounts to the new owners' names. A big mistake was to not do that in writing. Nor did we transfer the sales tax number, the utility accounts, or our Federal I.D. number—we planned to take care of those after the first year's anniversary. Another big mistake!

Everything appeared to go according to plan during the first month. We received our first payment and the rumblings from the crew that reached us we attributed to their adjusting to the new management. Midge and I, meanwhile, were recuperating from the grind of the last couple years.

But as the weeks passed, we received more news that the restaurant and staff morale were slipping. A couple suppliers also called complaining about late payments, and a friend at PG&E, the local utility, asked what was going on at the restaurant. He said a 24-hour notice was being sent out for unpaid electric bills.

Midge and I, ironically, were attending a personal improvement seminar in Los Angeles when Margie, our lead cook, called to tell me the staff's payroll checks were bouncing and that all hell was getting ready to break loose. I called the restaurant to tell Raul I would be in first thing in the morning to find out what was going on.

"Holy shit, what a disaster!" was all I could think to say the next morning. The kitchen was filthy. Most of the crew was milling around, demanding to have their checks made good. Customers were sparse.

Raul rolled into the parking lot an hour late in a brand new Cadillac. We grabbed some coffee and headed to the office, shutting the door behind us.

"What the fuck is going on?" were the first words out of my mouth. Raul began defending himself, insisting a bank error caused the bounced payroll checks. "Some error," I said, "if you don't deposit the money in the account you can't write the checks."

Sitting at my old desk, I happened to open the top drawer and discovered a stack of unopened mail more than two months old. Most was billing statements from suppliers, 24-hour notices from PG&E, sales tax reporting forms that needed to be filled out for payment, unemployment claims, and payment requests for services performed at the restaurant. The list was staggering! When I asked Raul to explain, he said the bookkeeper had been sick. Yeah, and the dog ate my homework.

I told Raul to pack up his stuff and get the hell out. In just three months, he had managed to ruin the good payment record we had established over many years. Even though we were struggling prior to his arrival, we always managed to pay the bills. New cars were a luxury in which we did not indulge.

Raul refused to leave, preaching that God would honor him and that I should pray for forgiveness for my aggressive behavior.

"I don't think God honors deceitful business practices carried out by someone under His banner," I replied. I wanted to shoot the bastard, I was so mad. The shock of the ignored bills had jerked me back to my senses.

We argued for hours. We both called our attorneys in an effort to gain the upper hand. Finally one of the cooks knocked on the door, cautiously opened it and asked if he should call the police. I instructed him to do so. The situation was very tense. Since I knew all the local cops, they asked me what they could do when they arrived. I explained the situation as best as I quickly could, asserted my legal ownership, and said I wanted Raul escorted out of the restaurant. With their persuasion, he finally left.

I spent the rest of the day—into the early hours of the morning—trying to make sense of where we were. I met with key members of the crew and explained I was back in charge and their pay checks would be made good. A cheer went up expressing their support, but we were a long way from being out of the woods.

RACK OF LAMB WITH A GARLIC/TOMATO REDUCTION AND DATE-FIG MINT JAM

Rack of lamb and lamb chops, like prime rib, lobster and New York strip steak, are menu standards. They show up on dinner menus across the nation and never seem to lose their appeal.

The French rack consists of eight ribs and weighs one and a half to two pounds. It is the "prime rib" of lamb. Much of today's supply is imported from Australia and New Zealand; however, the U.S. also produces some very high-quality lamb and many chefs prefer Colorado Lamb over the imports. "Frenched" is a butchering term that refers to removal of the fat and meat halfway down the rib bone, leaving the bone exposed.

A Note About Presentation

In restaurants, rack of lamb served and carved tableside can make for a spectacular presentation, especially when the rack comes planked and enveloped in a bouquetière of fresh vegetables and rosettes of duchess potatoes. Ideally, the waiter will carve the lamb by candlelight, serve a spoonful of mint demi-glaze over each chop, and offer guests their choice of vegetables and potatoes. Add a bottle of Syrah and the evening can hardly help but turn romantic.

Rack of Lamb with a Garlic/Tomato Reduction and Date-Fig Mint Jam

Ingredients:

Frenched rack of lamb	Dried dates
Garlic, chopped	Mint sprigs
All-purpose meat rub spice	Red chili peppers, dried
Butter	Mint jelly
Roma tomatoes, diced	Salt and pepper
White wine	Rosemary
Dried figs	

Remove any excess fat at the base of the rib bones of the Frenched rack or on the rib eye itself. Don't remove all the fat, as it's an important part of the cooking process, supplying flavor to the finished dish. Season with a dry all-purpose spice rub, or add salt and black pepper with a little rosemary. Rub the seasoning over the entire rack up to where the bones have been Frenched. If the rack is to be charbroiled, wrap the exposed bones in foil to protect them from blackening. If the lamb is to be roasted in the oven, the foil is not necessary.

Rack of Lamb with a Garlic/Tomato Reduction and Date-Fig Mint Jam (cont.)

If broiling outside on a barbeque grill, start the seasoned rack on the hot part of the fire and brown quickly on both sides. Then move it to a cooler part of the fire to finish cooking, which could take up to 40 minutes, depending on the barbeque. Ideal doneness is achieved at an internal temperature of 125 to 130 degrees for medium rare. Like most steak-cut meats, the rack should not be cooked to the well-done stage, which greatly reduces the dish's quality.

If roasting, place the seasoned rack in a hot oven at 425 degrees for the first five to ten minutes, until the meat browns. Reduce the temperature to 375 degrees to finish cooking, which will take approximately 20 minutes, or when the internal temperature reaches 125 to 130 degrees on a meat thermometer. It's important to insert the thermometer half way to the center of the thickest part of the eye to get an accurate reading. The reading should climb the scale steadily, and slow when reaching the desired level. If it climbs too fast, you'll likely over cook the lamb. Remember, the lamb will continue to cook a little after removing it from the oven or the broiler. Paying close attention to the lamb's temperature and how it rises can make all the difference.

When the rack reaches the desired temperature range, remove it from the heat and let it rest a couple of minutes before carving. To serve, cut four two-rib portions by running a sharp French knife between the bones and completely through the eye, creating beautiful medium-rare two-bone chops. Crisscross each two-bone pair in the center of a dinner plate to serve with your choice of side items.

In years past, lamb was always served with a small portion of mint jelly, a practice some restaurants still follow, but many more creative sauces and garnishes are available to enhance the flavor of this dish, including two of my favorites—a garlic and roma tomato reduction and date-fig mint jam.

Prepare the garlic and tomato reduction by warming half a stick of butter in a saucepan. Add eight cloves of chopped garlic and two diced roma tomatoes, also known as plum or Italian plum tomatoes. Cook down slightly, then add half a cup of white wine and reduce by half. Season with a little salt and pepper, and serve as a reduction or pureed to a velvety smoothness and ladled under the chops.

For the date-fig mint jam, place half a cup each of dried figs and dates in a food processor. Add a few sprigs of fresh mint and a teaspoon of dried red chilies, and blend into a paste. Stir in half a jar of mint jelly until the mixture acquires the consistency of jam. Thin, if necessary, with a little warm water, and serve on the side.

CHAPTER 18

THE DAY FROM HELL:
War and Weeds, and Something Worse

How many tickets are hanging?"

"Over 20 and still counting, and there's three take-out orders, not including the oil company's."

"I'll help out as soon as the parties are served," I told Margie. "Albert, get Sandy in here to pick up the next batch of salads for the baby shower." Sandy was one of the waitresses bussing the salad plates for the Kiwanis party. They were ready to serve the main course and were calling out from the pick-up side of the cook line.

"Now get back to the dishes and get caught up," I instructed Albert. Tubs of bussed plates were backing up, and the waitress station was out of clean silverware and glasses.

I plated-up the Kiwanis Club party myself. Since there wasn't time now to move the stir fry from the tilt skillet into hotel pans for service, I worked directly from the skillet, with the fire on low to keep the food hot. Nancy arrived for pick-up. Fortunately it was only a two-item plate—the stir fry and rice. I pulled a stack of warm plates from the oven, spreading out six at a time on the stainless steel table next to the tilt skillet, then placed the rice on one side of each plate and added the stir fry. Nancy could place the garnish on the side. All I had to do was repeat this process seven times and the main course would be served. Nancy could take care of the dessert by herself.

The kitchen was humming with activity. Albert was in high gear, scraping off bussed plates, soaking silverware, filling the dish racks, pre-spraying the plates, then slamming them home in the dishwasher, a not-so-glamorous but critically important part of any restaurant's operation. Without a steady flow of clean dishes, glasses and silverware, the service in the front of the house would come to a halt. The dishwasher also sanitizes the service ware. Keeping equipment clean and safe for our guests is vitally important. Many top cooks and chefs got their start washing dishes, just as I did.

I heard chatter coming from the cook line, which is not a good sign. When a cook line is in sync, there's little talk and no wasted motion, and to

DAY FROM HELL

a restaurant owner it's a beautiful thing to see. During peak service periods, plates are prepared at the rate of more than one a minute, quicker than in so-called fast food restaurants. Years later, when I was Executive Chef at Maison Jaussaud's, a large restaurant and lounge in Bakersfield, we would serve 400 to 500 dinners within a six-hour period on Saturday nights. An accomplishment like that is exhilarating, and after you've pulled it off, you sit down for a drink with fellow cooks, exhausted, but talking and laughing about how good the night's business was. (The wait staff is also dog tired but not so much so that they can't count their tips). These stressful days happen in busy establishments. Unfortunately, it creates fertile ground for other indulgences and questionable behavior. Many staff members communicate and share experiences more so with their co-workers than they do at home.

Even with the order terminal fixed, the pressure from serving the last-minute parties, while at the same time keeping up with the bigger-than-usual lunch crowd, began to take its toll. The exchanges between the cooks and wait staff became increasingly heated, and the natural rhythm of the line started to break down.

Things went from bad to worse. Waitresses were calling for orders that had been on the order wheel for over 30 minutes. Margie was doing her best, trying to keep the orders moving, but the order wheel was jammed with tickets, and a stack was waiting to be added. Finally, we got so backed up some of the tables were threatening to leave.

That was the last straw. Lunch, more than any other meal eaten away from home, requires quick service, especially for customers who have to return to work after their lunch breaks. No restaurant wants to be known for slow service. I needed to get back to the cook line and take charge as soon as I could, but that would have to wait till we finished serving the baby shower in the West Side Room.

Sandy had bussed the salad plates and we were ready to plate-up the Chicken Marsala—a three-item plate with a sauce for garnish. I set up a station to handle the plating myself. Sandy would have to ladle the sauce onto each plate before loading the plates on her service tray. I wanted to get this course served as quickly as possible so I could join the line cooks and help out. Sandy returned to pick up another six plates, only to tell me we had a rabbit in the group. Damn!

In restaurant jargon this little word means "vegetarian," a guest who requires special entrées to satisfy his or her dietary requirements. Depending on their persuasion, vegetarians may be adverse to any or all of the following: red meat of any kind, chicken, fish, wheat, lactose, flour, cheese, butter, eggs and genetically altered foods. The presence of the rabbit meant there would be a blip in the rhythm of my plate-up. We would have to serve the remainder of the baby shower and prepare the rabbit's entrée at the end.

"Check to see what foods on the planet she's able to eat," I told Sandy. "Suggest teaming something up with rice—we've got extra already made up."

"Will do."

"What's the verdict?" I asked Sandy when she came back in the kitchen after talking to the rabbit.

"She wants to know if the rice is made with animal stock." Of course it was. We used chicken stock to improve the rice's flavor. "Go back and tell her it is."

"The rice won't work, and fins or feathers won't either," Sandy reported back.

"Okay, if we have to, I'll sauté her a granola bar and garnish it with a shoot of bamboo from the planter out front. Hold on. There's a nice selection of fruits, vegetables and cottage cheese in the walk-in. Run it by her, and if it'll work, put it together. I've got to help the line cooks."

To vegetarians reading this (take the culinary world's characterization of you as a "rabbit" with a grain of salt), a word of advice: when attending functions where food will be served, if at all possible give the chef advance notice so he or she can prepare your dish. This will provide you with better service. Chefs really do want vegetarians to enjoy their meals along with everyone else.

I dreaded having to jump into the maelstrom on the cook line, but it was unavoidable. Conditions had deteriorated. What I was seeing was far more serious than merely being in the weeds. We had moved beyond the next phase, a train wreck, and had progressed all the way to a—I hate to use such a term, but no other word captures it as fully—a cluster fuck. And we were experiencing it in its most virulent form, a full-blown cluster fuck, an FBCF.

A chef or line cook never forgets going through an FBCF. A regular CF thankfully leaves your memory a week or so after the event, but an FBCF is a different story. I have had the misfortune of living through several of them, and have never forgotten where they happened and when, or the faces of the poor bastards who were swept up in them. To this day, those memories can twist my stomach into a knot.

When you're in the middle of an FBCF, everything is hitting the fan. Chefs' jackets become unrecognizably soiled from kitchen spills, aprons turn greasy, kitchen towels look like they came from an auto shop, fingers get cut and curse words flow like chocolate ganache. The cursing, like the ganache, floats like a topping over the din of total chaos.

A FBCF is being up to your ass in alligators and unable to focus on draining the swamp. And that's where our cooks were when I re-joined the line. "Where the hell are we?" I asked. No one knew. The waitresses were in panic mode, screaming for their table pick-ups, most of which were way past the limit for prompt service. Not being my first CF, I knew this would be a good time to just stop everything. That may sound counterproductive, but taking stock of where we were was the only chance for the cooks to regroup and maybe, only *maybe*, save the rest of the day.

The Trimmings

Thanksgiving-style turkey dinners are typically served with cranberry sauce, sweet potatoes, a vegetable such as French-cut green beans topped with crisp fried onion pieces, fresh rolls and pumpkin pie with whipped cream. I leave such additions to the reader's creativity. Over the years, students in my cooking classes have told me my way of preparing the Thanksgiving dinner saves time and lowers the stress of making it without compromising the result. "In all the years I've been preparing Thanksgiving dinners," one student wrote me, "the past year was the easiest and earned me more compliments about everything. I even got to enjoy interacting with my guests." Try it, it works.

TRADITION MADE EASY—THANKSGIVING TURKEY WITH ONE-POT MASHED POTATOES

Growing up, Thanksgiving Day turkey was an all day affair for my mom, the one meal she always went the extra mile to please her brood of seven children. She would start by laying in supplies days in advance, and begin meal prep the day before. On Thanksgiving Day, she was in the kitchen by 6 a.m.

She used no recipe books and chased us from the kitchen whenever we interrupted by trying to sneak a taste. I always tried to sample the chewy dressing or peel a piece of crisp skin off the breast of the roasted bird. I'm not sure if she considered it a labor of love or just another motherly duty. Either way, it was a tremendous amount of work.

Professional chefs find it almost impossible to duplicate the home-cooked turkey dinner mothers prepare over the years. Family traditions, the presence of familiar relatives and friends, unique or unusual local foods and the holiday ambience create an atmosphere and a meal that can only be experienced at home.

Despite all this, I consider preparing a turkey dinner one of my specialties. I'm not trying to compete with mom's meal, but a year's experience working at the White Turkey Inn in Hamden, Connecticut, helped me bring a little scratch to the game. Turkey dinner was an everyday menu item at the Inn, and not reserved for holidays. As a result, I've prepared and served thousands of turkey dinners over the span of my 50-year career. What follows is not a recipe, but suggestions about preparation and cooking methods to make the task easier and help produce a better, tastier bird.

First, there's no escaping the fact that preparing a traditional turkey dinner is a lot of work. The shopping list can be as long as your arm and, inevitably, leads to additional trips to the store for missed items. Step one, therefore is to spend a little time creating a thorough list.

Thanksgiving Turkey with One-Pot Mashed Potatoes

Ingredients

2 turkeys

Celery

Carrots

Onions

Corn bread

Toasted croutons

Sausage

Butter

Russet potatoes, peeled and quartered

Flour

Salt

Black pepper

Sour cream

Heavy cream

Presidents these days like to pardon two turkeys for Thanksgiving. I like to cook two. I always purchase two turkeys and roast and bone out the smaller one a day or two before the dinner. This provides the necessary bones and drippings to prepare a good turkey stock that I use to make the gravy and dressing, and to keep sliced turkey meat moist and hot. If you purchase two birds, wrap the larger one and stick it in the refrigerator soon as you arrive home. The first is your insurance you will have enough meat to take care of everyone's appetites—including the family chowhounds, of which every gathering has at least one—and extra white and dark meat for sandwiches and other leftovers.

Before roasting either bird, I remove from its cavities the neck, gizzard, heart and liver, and set them aside. I wash the bird in cold water and season it inside and out with salt and pepper. Next, I place the whole bird in a roasting pan, rubbing it all over with any salad oil except olive oil, and slide it into a 325-degree oven. The weight of the bird determines its roasting time. I allow approximately 15 minutes per pound. A 16-pound bird, unstuffed, requires about 3 ½ to 4 hours of cooking time. For the last 20 minutes, increase the temperature of the oven to 400 degrees to nicely brown the skin. During roasting, it's also helpful to baste the bird with some turkey stock.

Thanksgiving Turkey with One-Pot Mashed Potatoes (cont.)

The turkey can be covered and uncovered, as needed, with aluminum foil during the roasting process. If the turkey includes a pop-up doneness button, that eliminates much of the guesswork. Alternatively, you can insert a meat thermometer in the thickest part of the thigh and breast and look for an internal temperature of 160 degrees. Fully cooked, the bird should show a little shrinkage of the breast and the thighs pulling slightly away from the cavity.

Boning a cooked turkey is not a big deal. Be not afraid. After roasting, let it cool slightly, then remove the breast and thigh meat in large pieces. Strip the drumsticks as best you can, and toss the scraps and trim into the stock for extra flavor. The goal is to remove as much usable meat as possible. Of utmost importance, save the drippings! Pan drippings, also called fond, contain an incredible amount of flavor.

A good stock is essential and can easily be prepared with the rest of the meal. I make the stock by adding to a stockpot turkey bones and the pan drippings of the first roasted turkey, a mirepoix which consists of celery, carrots and onions, and enough water to cover it. I season the stock to taste with a few crushed peppercorns, fresh parsley and little thyme and sage, then simmer it for several hours. I also throw in the onion peels for color and flavor and skim the stock frequently, saving any fat I remove.

After starting the stock, I take the innards I've reserved and wash them, then simmer them in a pan of water until tender. Next, I remove and strip the meat off the necks, dice the liver and heart, saving the meat for the gravy preparation. I add the neck bones and the trim from the innards into the stock.

The finished stock, usually obtained in 3 to 6 hours, should display a golden color and possess an intense turkey flavor. Commercially, we let stocks simmer overnight and strain them first thing in the morning. If you choose to do this, be sure the stockpot has enough water to keep it from simmering dry.

When the stock is ready, strain it fully along with any remaining turkey fat that rises to the top. Letting the stock cool, I refrigerate it for use the next day. Sometimes I refill the pot with water to make a second batch. Even if I end up with extra stock, I always find uses for it, in soups, gravies, croquettes and turkey a la king to cite a few examples. It can also be frozen for later use.

On Thanksgiving Day, remove the stock from the refrigerator and skim the congealed fat off the top. Place the fat in a bowl to use later for the dressing and giblet gravy. Put the stock back on the stove to simmer. Wash

Thanksgiving Turkey with One-Pot Mashed Potatoes (cont.)

and season the second turkey, and place it in the oven for roasting.

I like to use corn bread and toasted croutons for the dressing. You may prefer a ready-made dressing mix complete with seasoning. Some very good ones, like those from Stove Top, Orowheat and Pepperidge Farm, are on the market. If you would rather make your own, begin by sautéing some onions, celery and sausage. Add the corn bread and croutons, and season. Moisten with hot turkey stock, melted butter and a little melted turkey fat. Add any other ingredients you prefer, or that are traditional to your family. The key is to use a good stock and turkey fat to improve the flavor.

I do not recommend stuffing the bird prior to roasting. This might be a common practice, but it adds more time to the roasting and can cause food poisoning from bacterial growth if not removed at the completion of cooking. The giblet gravy has to be just right, and since it's used on at least three items in the meal—the turkey, the dressing and the mashed potatoes, make sure there's enough. Begin by straining hot turkey fat into a saucepan and melting into it one or two sticks of butter, depending on the size of the pan. With a French whip, whisk in flour over a low heat to make a smooth roux, using equal parts of flour and fat. After slightly cooking the roux, begin adding hot turkey stock, briskly whisking to form a thin paste, and work out any flour lumps.

Next, add enough stock to create the consistency of gravy, whisking all the while. The thickening power of the roux becomes apparent when the gravy reaches a boil. At this point, cut back to low heat. Stir in the chopped giblets and chopped neck meat, taste for seasoning, and set aside for service. If it thickens further as it sits, add more stock to thin it down a bit.

You can continue to keep the meal simple with my One-Pot Mashed Potatoes. Start by boiling several peeled and quartered russet potatoes in a large pot. How many will depend on the size of your guest list. One large potato usually makes enough mashed potatoes for two to three normal servings. When the potatoes are tender enough to break apart if pierced by a fork, they're ready for mashing.

Strain off the water and leave the potatoes in the pot, seasoning them with a little salt and black pepper. Break up the potatoes with a heavy French whip while adding a stick of butter, a little sour cream and heavy cream to smooth the mixture to the right consistency. Whisk it enough to remove lumps, but not so much that you create a potato paste. This should take no more than a couple of minutes, but has to be done while the potatoes are still piping hot.

Thanksgiving Turkey with One-Pot Mashed Potatoes (cont.)

Taste the potatoes for seasoning, then transfer them from the pot to an oven-proof serving dish, top with a couple pats of butter to keep them from crusting, set the dish into the oven, and reheat it just before serving. There should be no bowls or electric beaters to clean when finished—just one pot.

At this point, the refrigerated first turkey can be sliced, placed in a casserole with a couple of ladles of hot turkey stock, and reheated to be served moist and tender. When it's finished roasting, the second turkey can be carved tableside or deboned as you prefer. If deboned, you can prepare another stock for future use.

CHAPTER 19

Apocalypse Part II

The management contract with Raul and his wife had been cancelled and they were sent packing, but there was still a lot of unfinished business. I called the pastor of the church in Southern California, filling him in on the actions of one of his flock. His conversation was guarded. I sensed this incident with Raul might not have been the first trouble he had gotten into. The pastor inquired how much Raul owed on the debt at Leonard's. When I told him nearly $100,000 incurred in just three months, he was shocked. He suggested I come to the church to meet with the deacons and Raul to discuss a solution.

My friend Chuck and I headed south to meet with the pastor, five deacons, and Raul. We exchanged the usual pleasantries, except for Raul and myself. I began by dropping the stack of unpaid bills at Raul's feet and asking why they had not been paid. I also asked what happened to the thousands of dollars from restaurant sales. Raul jumped up from his seat to confront me and Chuck had to physically hold me back because I wanted to tear the guy's head off.

The meeting went on like this for a couple of heated hours. At one point, I grew so angry I tried to pick up a Remington bronze from a side table with every intention of letting Raul have it. The deacons tackled me before I could get a good grip on the piece. The end result was that Raul would begin paying $300 per month on the debt as restitution. The pastor drew up an agreement and we both signed it.

The pastor's agreement could have been written on toilet paper, as it was worthless. Raul made two payments then bounced the third. No further checks were received and the pastor no longer took my calls. I later learned I was not the first restaurateur Raul had defrauded. By then, I was done with Raul and could no longer afford to waste more time and energy trying to hold him accountable.

Meanwhile I'd gone back to the grind, in worse shape than ever financially. Midge could not bring herself to return to the restaurant and we both agreed her time would be better spent taking care of our two children, Shelly and Greg. Quickly, the bad news began to sink in. Raul's three-month reign had put the restaurant in arrears close to $100,000 on top of the existing debt service on the loan. The money problem seemed insurmountable. I met with our CPA to discuss options and his advice was to file for bankruptcy. Our attorney offered the same advice. Returning to my office, I sat at my desk with the lights turned out and thought about all the mistakes I had made that had landed me in this mess.

The following morning, I called my attorney to let him know I wanted to hold off on the bankruptcy filing. He insisted that bankruptcy was my best option. I said I wanted to take a shot at working my way out of the hole.

I had a plan to bring Leonard's back from the brink. First, I listed all of Leonard's creditors and the amounts owed them on a legal-size yellow pad that had filled every line of three pages. The food suppliers had already stopped shipping to us and were, by far, the largest group on the list. It made no difference that I had alerted them about the change in restaurant management. Although sympathetic, they argued that my name was still tied to the account and I was responsible for the debt. This was the price of not having notified them in writing.

My plan included negotiating a lesser payment with each creditor for the monies owed. Most agreed to forgive the interest and penalties, but everyone wanted their principal paid in full. I always asked why they let my accounts fall so far behind. Their replies amazed me. Almost all—including the State Board of Equalization and PG&E—said my record had been so good over the years they were willing to give me extra leeway on late payments. Everyone had ignored my phone call about transferring their account to the new owners so that all my years of stellar performance actually helped create the current situation.

With food shipments suspended, I was forced to purchase food and supplies at the Costco store 35 miles away in Bakersfield, and pay for them in cash at the time of purchase. This meant almost daily 70-mile round trip runs to Bakersfield. I transported everything back to the restaurant in the rear seat and trunk of my car. It was quite a sight to see Chef Len rumbling down the road in a car so full of groceries it resembled a low rider.

Day by day, week after week, I soldiered on, yellow pad at hand, slowly nibbling down the debt. Besides the creditors, approximately $14,000 in bounced checks had to be addressed. I contacted the D.A. to see about making Raul the responsible party since his signature was on the checks. No luck. The larger creditors sued me, and I had to navigate my way through seven law suits, spending precious time and energy resolving debts I was trying to pay off in the first place.

I heard the words "You're served" more than I wish to remember. Collection calls and letters and process servers became a regular part of my routine. The process servers would come into the kitchen, walk up to me, ask my name, then tap me with a document, and walk away as it fell to the floor. This was a bitter pill to swallow. Once, I tried to have a little fun with the process. I was at the meat grinder preparing sausage when one of these guys came up to me looking for Leonard.

"Has anyone seen Leonard?" I bellowed out to the rest of the cooks as I looked up. Amid widespread laughter, I pointed the process server to the coffee pot and suggested he get a cup of coffee while I tried to find Leonard. I quickly poured myself a cup and confessed that I was his man. Even he laughed.

Each evening, I would take the day's receipts and go through a rationing process, setting aside money for current expenses, payroll, and our household expenses. Any remainder went to paying down the debt. Months passed and my yellow pad was filling with lines drawn through the names of creditors who had been paid off. The yellow pad was my scorecard and the symbol of my progress.

After eighteen long, grueling months, I drew a line through the last creditor's name. Those debts had been paid off in full! My CPA and attorney both said it was a miracle. I really don't know how we got through it.

Leonard's was again on a firm footing. We'd regained the top spot in town, re-established our supplier accounts, brought the restaurant loan current without Taft National losing a penny, and restored my reputation. I could hold my head up again.

Burning out in any business can not only have serious consequences, but teach critical lessons. I learned, painfully, that I needed more time for my family, which then included Midge and our children, Shelly and Greg. Prior to Leonard's, I thought no sacrifice too big for the sake of my business. I learned this is not true. When you sacrifice your family and yourself, you need to find a better way of doing things.

Shortly after Charlie Reid pulled his signature off our loan, throwing our finances into chaos, Midge and I found ourselves sitting in the parking lot of the Cottage Hospital in Santa Barbara. We had learned Charlie was suffering from cancer and was in the late stages of the disease. He was our angel at the start of Leonard's, but the loan issues had strained our friendship. We sat in the car at least half an hour discussing what we should say when we saw him. I was worried he might find our visit upsetting.

Charlie was the guy who walked into Leonard's while it was under construction and asked me how everything was going. At that point, we had completed about 90 percent of the remodel and were ready to install the kitchen equipment and dining room furniture.

Everything was fine, I replied from my perch on a five-gallon plastic bucket having a cup of coffee. But Charlie sensed the strain in my voice and pressed me further. That's when I admitted we had spent close to $200,000 and had yet to secure a loan for the equipment package. The equipment was sitting in a warehouse in Oakland, I told him, waiting to be shipped.

How much did we need to make the shipment happen, Charlie asked. I was blunt, $75,000 for the equipment in Oakland and $125,000 for additional equipment to be shipped from the East Coast. Charlie asked if I had the phone number for the distributor in Oakland. "Sure," I replied.

"Good," said Charlie. "Call and let them know the money will be wired today, and to get that fucking equipment on a truck headed our way."

Hardly believing my luck, I offered to pay Charlie a couple points on the loan.

"You owe me nothing other than to prepare abalone for me once in awhile in the back kitchen," he responded. We shook hands, which was how such things were done in 1983.

I asked Charlie why he'd take on so much liability to help us fund Leonard's.

"Very simple," he said, "you're a hard worker with a great track record here. I know you'll make it good."

Sitting in the car, we realized how much faith Charlie had put in us. Now, we were getting ready to visit him on his deathbed. Finally, we left the car and made our way to his room. I felt myself trembling when we walked in. Charlie started crying as we approached. He looked frail, he had lost a lot of weight, and his skin color was ashen. The cancer had wreaked havoc on him.

"I'm sorry for pulling my signature," were the first words out of his mouth. He said he had done so chiefly because he did not want to leave his family with the added liability of our note. At this point, the negative input from Paul and Cindy didn't really matter. Midge and I both replied we totally understood. The conversation lightened then and soon we were laughing about abalone dinners I had cooked and how I had made him feel like a V.I.P. with his own personal chef.

"Charlie, you are our V.I.P.," and all of us started crying. We knew how much we would miss him. Charlie passed away just a week after our visit, a visit that began with us afraid to leave the car.

Unfortunately, Paul and Cindy divorced within a year of returning to Delaware. A few years later, Paul was diagnosed with stomach cancer and given six months to live. I flew back and visited with him at my mother's home in Claymont, Delaware.

Mending fences, we forgave each other over our partnership differences and talked about the challenges of growing up in our family.

I don't believe our father ever understood or appreciated Paul's entrepreneurial ability. He always criticized him for working in seasonal businesses. But those businesses supported his family. Dad's idea of a good job was to work at DuPont, as he did. The only times I witnessed Paul and dad get along were when they played music together. Paul was a good trumpet player and Dad respected that.

Paul taught me how to work at a very young age. Even at 11, he was always finding things for me to do in his rotating businesses. He played a big role in teaching me the value of a good work ethic, and I picked up on his entrepreneurial spirit.

Later in life, Paul became more cynical and negative, and often just wanted to be alone. The restaurant business did not fit him well. I think he realized that and chose to escape to the freedom of the open road by driving trucks cross-country. The years had beaten him up. At the end, he said he'd lived a hard, tough life and was tired. It became obvious he was ready to go. He elected to forego any further cancer treatments other than morphine for pain. He was 52 years old when he passed.

ABALONE AMBITIONS

I drive north from Morro Bay, nine miles along Highway 1 to buy abalone, a key ingredient in one of my favorite special dishes. Abalone has been cherished for centuries for its delicate flavor, beautiful shell and, among believers, its aphrodisiac qualities.

The drive to the Abalone Farm (www.abalonefarm.com) on the north end of Cayucos at Estero Point, along some of the most scenic coastline in California, is as wonderful as the succulent mullosk I'm procuring. Turning left off Route 1, I soon detect the smell of wild sage and rosemary. Cresting the last steep hill of a winding, bumpy dirt road, the farm comes into view. Scores of cement salt water tanks filled with kelp and abalone stretch across the tops of the cliffs above the crashing waves of the blue Pacific below.

The Abalone Farm is the oldest and largest producer of farm-raised abalone in the U.S. It produces more than 5 million California Red Abalone (haliotis rufescens) per year, which it supplies to restaurants and ships all over the world. If I arrive during lunch, I may catch a soccer game between teams made up of the farm's largely Hispanic work force. Brad, the General Manager, usually meets me in the lower parking area, from which we ascend to the production building to pick up my order.

In the production area, six to eight women seated at worktables and armed with tenderizing mallets pound away at the abalone flesh to make it tender enough to eat. Brad usually reaches between the flailing mallets to grab a couple small steaks for us to sample sashimi style. After dipping them in a mixture of rice vinegar, soy sauce and red chili oil, we down the delicious slices with a quick chew.

Recipe Note

In 2012, I was hired as guest chef for a video shoot in Monterey, California, to introduce Dreaming Tree Everyday, a new wine varietal brought out by Dave Matthews of the Dave Matthews Band. I prepared Sautéed Abalone for Dave and his winemaker as part of the shoot. Dave said it was one of the best things he had ever eaten.

I like to sauté abalone when I'm not using it for sashimi or sushi. Preparing Sautéed Abalone is very simple; however, the timing is critical. Chris Jones, a long-time friend, taught it to me more than 40 years ago. Chris liked to dive for wild abalone at a time when they were still plentiful along the Central Coast.

Sauteéd Abalone

Ingredients

Abalone

Eggs

Saltine crackers

Clarified butter

Lemon

Begin with pounded pieces of abalone steak. Dip them in whole beaten eggs, then place them in crushed saltine crackers, breading the abalone on both sides. To sauté, bring clarified butter up to temperature. Place the abalone steaks in a large pan, taking care not to crowd them. Lightly brown the steaks, approximately 40 seconds per side. At the last minute, squeeze a fresh lemon over them and serve immediately, ladling a little of the now browned-butter over them. Any overcooking will cause the abalone to toughen and dry.

What I like about the dish is its simplicity. There's no reason to even accompany it with a sauce. The light cracker crust seals in the abalone's delicate flavor. We serve the dish on our charter yacht, the Papagallo II, and always to rave reviews.

CHAPTER 20

THE DAY FROM HELL:
What? No Fries? And Other Felonies

Before anything else, I had to check with the waitresses to see how many tables were threatening to walk out, and prevent that from happening. This had to be done tactfully, because waitresses can favor regular customers by moving their orders to the front. After all, for the wait staff it's all about the tips, their real pay check.

I pulled the tickets that had been waiting the longest for pick-up, and instructed the waitresses to apologize to the guests for the delays, using whatever excuse they could come up with to placate them. Yes, being lied to is sometimes part of the dining experience. Next, I assumed the role of the wheel man.

I much prefer working the broiler station, but a chef must be able to perform any duty in the kitchen—and an owner, any job in the entire operation. A good wheel man directs the rhythm and pace of the line and makes things happen. He or she also acts as the go-between among the wait staff and cooks.

Our 310-seat restaurant was large enough to support specific stations on the line—sauté, broiler, pantry and fry. When an order comes in, the wheel man cries out, "ordering," and singles out the menu items for the various stations. Each station cook then begins preparing the menu items he or she is responsible for. Several minutes go by before the wheel man shouts "fire" for the table that's ready to go, followed by the final call, "pick-up," for the table just fired.

The wheel man can be likened to a symphony conductor and the wait staff and cooks to the members of his orchestra. During peak periods, the wheel man's voice can be heard constantly barking out the commands of "ordering…firing…pick-up." Seasoned cooks need only glance at the tickets, and can complete the steps just by hearing them called out. I'm sure you've heard the expression, "It's all about the timing," and just as in a musical performance, timing is essential to a restaurant's operation. It works most of the time, but there are days when it doesn't.

DAY FROM HELL

The take-out waitress asked for the oil company's order. There were several oil companies in and around Taft, and this particular one was one of our largest customers, doing several thousand dollars worth of business with us every year. Their order had to move now. "Where are we on this one?" I asked, and was happy to hear that it was complete, bagged and ready, except for two cheeseburgers "dragging" from the broiler. Dragging allows us to move a partially completed order and have wait staff come back for the remaining items when they are ready. It works if the dragged items can be plated in a minute or two, but not if it takes ten or fifteen. The longer an item drags, the greater the danger the order will be picked up with an item missing. "Okay, move that order to the take-out window, but be sure to put a hold on it until the burgers are done."

With the oil company's order out of the way, we began to slowly close in on the backlog of the other orders, and the normal rhythm of the line gradually began to return. The worst seemed to be behind us.

To reduce the order backlog even further, I risked another tactic: sandwiching the service for tables of two or three diners between the larger orders, regardless of who came first. Food for parties of two or three can be prepared easily, so we could move them ahead of a larger group that was not quite ready to go. Then we would have one or two less tickets to worry about, clearing the way for new incoming orders.

But there's a down side to this—if a group at a larger table sees food being served to a two or three-person party that arrived after they did, things can turn sour in a hurry. While the folks at the smaller table are delighted, the group at the larger table quickly begins complaining about how they've been slighted.

"We were here first! How did they get served ahead of us? We're starving and they pull this on us! Where's the manager? No, the owner! I want to see the owner—now!"

Of course, that poor soul is me. Usually in such a situation I'll offer a complimentary bottle of wine or a round of drinks to tide the table over until the food arrives, and it usually works. The slight is quickly forgotten, and I've learned to never underestimate the power of a freebie.

Three "two tops" (tables for two) were mixed in with the larger orders. "Fire and pick-up Tables 6, 11 and 20," I barked, referring to the orders that could be finished quickly, and crossed my fingers that we would get away with it, that any would-be grumblers and complainers in the larger parties would not notice that they were being bypassed.

Out of the blue, our fry cook said we were low on French fries. "What the hell? Where's the backup?" I fumed. Our fries were made fresh using a French fry cutter. Once cut, the fries were washed, blanched and chilled in the walk-in cooler to be ready for frying when ordered. French fries are absolutely indispensable, the one menu item no chef ever wants to run out of, especially during the busy lunch hour when so many of the menu items are served with them.

"Augie, didn't you check for backup this morning?" I asked our breakfast and lunch cook.

"With all that was going on in the kitchen I forgot."

Again, the importance of *mise en place*. French fries were just too important to "86," (chef speak for running out of an item) and without them, the waitresses would have to return to their tables and ask for substitutes. "Albert, start with 10 pounds of potatoes, run them through the French fry cutter, and get them to Augie for blanching."

"What about the dishes and silverware?"

"Albert, just do it!"

The shortage of French fries put us back in the weeds, just as we were about to climb out. Janet, one of the waitresses, came back to the cook line with more news from the front: "The lady at Table 7 is here with eight guests from the Bay Area and she's very disappointed our large fried-prawn platter isn't available."

"What do you mean it's not available? That's one of our signature items!"

"After we sold out in the lunch rush, Margie 86'ed it."

I motioned for Margie to come over, and asked her how many orders we started with.

"We had six breaded and ready to go," she answered.

The fried prawn platter was more of a dinner item, and we usually didn't move more than one or two at lunch. Today, the whole world wanted it. "I thought we could get by, but we had a run on them," Margie explained, "and with everything else we had to do, there wasn't enough time to prepare more."

When a menu item is low, you take the chance you'll make it through the peak service period with what's on hand. It never fails, it's the culinary version of Murphy's Law—the item that's low is the item that gets ordered the most! If you prepare more before the rush, no one orders it! More often than not, the item you run out of requires a lot more prep time, too. That's how this little rule works—why would it be any different today?

"How many orders did they want?" I asked.

"Everyone at the table ordered it after the lady told them how good it was and that it was a specialty of the house."

"So that's nine orders?"

"No, ten. Her husband's with them and wants the shrimp, too. When you get a chance, they asked if you could come out and say hello."

"Let them know we're jammed up in the kitchen, but I'll try my best," I said. After all, what else did I have to do?

"Len, you're a doll. Thanks for making it happen. They'll be so pleased."

She'll get a good tip out of this one, and I was happy for her. I love it when our staff does well, even when my butt's getting kicked.

"Margie, take over the wheel. I'm going to knock out the shrimp orders. Please tell me we have enough coleslaw to handle the sides."

"We do."

"Keep the French fry blanching going to catch us up," I told her as she took the wheel.

The shrimp were one of our best sellers, very popular with the locals. We used only the finest available, and prepared them fresh. We began with U-10 Mexican White Shrimp, meaning from the Gulf of Mexico and large—no more than 10 shrimp per pound.

Each day we peeled, de-veined and butterflied them before breading them in a special blend of crumbs made from dinner rolls and fresh sourdough bread. Before placing the shrimp in the breading, we tossed the cleaned shrimp in seasoned flour, which insulates the shrimp during frying, then dipped them into beaten eggs to bind them to the breadcrumbs. This was SBP (standard breading procedure), one of the first things cooks learn. Properly breaded and fried in clean oil at the right temperature, the blended crumbs create a tasty, delicate crust that encases the shrimp, making a beautiful, light golden-brown product, free of any greasy taste or texture.

During prep, it's a good idea to keep one hand free of the egg mixture and reserve it for the flour and breading, otherwise you'll end up breading your fingers. This is a common mistake made by inexperienced cooks, or a cook in a hurry, like yours truly. After completing the SBP, my fingers looked like I was wearing work gloves—if I dipped them in the hot oil they would come out looking like ten corn dogs. The pot and pan sink served for a quick cleanup.

"Augie, here's the shrimp for the Table 7 ticket. Get it fried and ready for plate-up. Margie, did you get the rest of those take-out orders moved?"

"They're gone."

"Good. Where are we on the rest of the orders?"

"Albert caught us up on the fries, and when Augie moves the ten top with the shrimp, we'll be down to just six tickets."

"Great!" The lunch rush was winding down.

"Len, we have a five top in with three more orders of shrimp." Murphy's Law again. Back I went to the breading station.

Next up was cleaning the line and prepping for the night crew. "Margie, get some rest breaks in for the cooks, then start on the prep and backup for the night cooks."

With that out of the way, I could go out and say hello to the lady at Table 7 and her guests. I put on a clean chef's coat, and went out to meet them.

"Hi, I'm Len," I said when I got to their table.

"Jean," the lady smiled, "and this is my husband, Arthur."

"Call me Art," her husband said as he got up to shake my hand. "Pleased to meet you."

"Same here," I said, shaking Art's hand. "You folks are from the Bay Area?"

"We lived in Sausalito until Art got transferred to Taft about three years ago. Lovely place," Jean answered.

By "lovely place" she must mean Sausalito, and he must work for one of the oil companies, I thought.

"Our guests are all former neighbors," the lady went on. "We're having a reunion of sorts," she smiled. And some guests they were! Right before me were three beautiful girls that had to be in their early twenties. It was hard to keep my eyes off of them. I took a deep breath and let it out. Maybe this day wasn't *entirely* from hell, after all.

Foxes and Wolves

I would be remiss not to mention the buzz that travels between waiters and cooks, a largely male fraternity, checking out the babes among their female guests. Word would often get back to us in the kitchen when a fox was sighted at a particular table. The cooks would find any excuse to wander by the table and grab a gander. Their check-out list would include the hemlines of skirts, long legs, exposed cleavage, hair colors and styles, even eye color.

Holidays were often the liveliest such occasions. During Mother's Day, the restaurant was abloom with eye candy of every size and description, women diners splendidly decked out in the bright colors of spring. It was a babe-watching bonanza. Beautiful women stirred the staff's passions like great food, fine wines, and chocolate stirred the passions of their guests. The joy and appreciation the male waiters and cooks felt for their customers of the opposite sex was so strong, it reminded me of the song lyric "nature's way of giving, a reason to be living."

I know this sounds sexist but, hey, I didn't make me. The blood that courses through my veins is just passing through on its evolutionary journey. I love and cherish women. I also love my wife with the additional feelings of respect, caring, loyalty, and companionship she inspires. I'm proud to have her with me. But I'm also still a guy.

This side of the cooking life had a profound effect on my career choice when I was 14 years old and working my first real job in a restaurant. I knew early on I was not college material, although I had graduated from the Culinary Institute of America after high school. My skills and temperament were always more suited to a career in the trades. I got to eat what I wanted, I did not have to shine academically, I got paid and, the best part, the restaurant work attracted girls. As a result, I never wasted much time checking out other career options.

113

A SAINT PATRICK'S SPECIAL—CORNED BEEF, CABBAGE AND VEGGIES

In Ireland, before the advent of refrigeration, beef corned before winter was served in the spring with freshly harvested green cabbage, making for a stick-to-your-ribs feast. Many cooks prepare this as a one-pot meal. I prefer to cook the ingredients separately to avoid over or under cooking any one ingredient and to better preserve the food's colors.

As I do with Thanksgiving turkey, I cook the corned beef the day before, which also provides a stock for cooking the vegetables. I use a corned beef brisket that comes vacuum-sealed in brine, either from Real McCoy or Bill Baileys Irish Brand. I use one or the other every year, while some chefs prefer to brine their own briskets several weeks ahead.

Corned Beef, Cabbage and Veggies

Ingredients:

Corned beef brisket, vacuum-sealed in brine
Celery
White onions, peeled and quartered
Carrots, peeled and quartered
Russet potatoes, peeled and quartered
Green cabbage
Pickling spices
Horseradish
Mustard
Worcestershire sauce

Begin by removing the brisket from its sealed package, saving the liquid and seasoning that comes with it. Add all three to a large stockpot filled with water and bring it to a boil. Add celery, onion and additional pickling spice, and reduce the heat to a simmer. Beef brisket is a tougher cut that requires several hours of cooking to become tender. This so-called moist heat method transfers the heat from the flavored stock to the meat. The brisket is tender when you can stick a kitchen fork into its thickest part and easily remove it.

When tender, move the brisket to a tray to cool, and strain off the stock for later use. Trim off most of the fat, leaving some for flavor. If not serving that day, cover and refrigerate the beef overnight.

Corned Beef, Cabbage and Veggies (cont.)

For vegetables, I use carrots, white onions, russet potatoes, all peeled and quartered, and green cabbage. The cabbage should be washed, trimmed, cut in half, cored, and cut into wedges. Simmer the carrots and potatoes together in the stock until tender, being careful not to overcook them to the point they turn mushy and fall apart.

Next, arrange the raw onion sections and cabbage wedges in a high-sided pan or pot. Pour boiling stock over them and cover the pan with foil, letting the onions and cabbage steep in the hot liquid. This is usually enough to cook them while keeping the onions white and the cabbage a bright green. If you find they're not done enough, place them over a fire a few minutes. Again, don't over cook, as the cabbage will fade from a nice fresh looking green to a wilted brown.

Slice the corned beef across the grain then lay the slices out in a pan covered with hot stock. When all the ingredients have finished cooking, arrange the items on individual plates, or on a large platter, family style, for the guests to help themselves. Accompany the meal with a hot mustard dip made using one part prepared horseradish, three parts hot, spicy mustard and a few shakes of Worcestershire sauce. Use the dip as a condiment for the brisket.

CHAPTER 21

Mother's Day

After Midge and I sold Leonard's, I dabbled in a couple of other fields, the result of which was to quickly exhaust our proceeds from the sale. Then I bounced back into the restaurant industry, taking the Executive Chef position at Maisson Jaussauds, a landmark restaurant in Bakersfield.

One of the easiest ways to get into trouble in the food business is to claim you're skilled enough to do certain jobs you've never done before. (The best advice I give a new cook is to never pretend you can do something if you really don't know how. If the chef asks you to prepare a certain dish, sauce, or garnishing technique and you don't know how, admit it and ask to be shown. You'll be better off than trying to fake it.)

I had to learn this the hard way. In my case, the error was taking on a buffet project for which I was totally unprepared. I had done plenty of buffets, but none on the scale—in staff, supplies, and equipment—to which I had naively agreed. Ironically, my one-man crash and burn, both exhausting and unexpected, was from the perspectives of the restaurant owner and the diners in attendance a great success. The memory of it, however, still stings whenever I think of it.

The disaster occurred, incongruously, on Mother's Day, a sunny Sunday in 1992 at Maison Jaussaud's, an 18,000-square-foot restaurant and entertainment lounge. Mother's Day was the year's single busiest day. All hands were expected to be on deck. No staff had the day off, even to take out their own mothers.

The owner, the general manager and myself had decided to offer a Grand Buffet, a project familiar to me but never at the scale we were envisioning. The idea was to streamline the ordering process while maximizing our seating and turnover rates. People would come in, the hostess would seat them, the wait staff would take beverage orders and the guests would saunter through the buffet, selecting foods and stopping at any of the several cooking stations. I was Maison Jaussaud's Executive Chef, the man in charge of the back of the house. I was where the buck stopped for anything concerning food, the kitchen staff, and operations.

Buffet service is popular and usually fairly easy to maintain throughout a meal service. But for this Mother's Day, Jim, the owner, wanted to pull out all the stops, and was willing to put his money where his mouth was. Spare no expense, he said. He wanted to make a statement, and did. The set-up was incredible.

We had spent most of the week leading up to the big day preparing food. No question about it, this was going to be the best Mother's Day buffet in the city. Fully skirted tables snaked through our Club Room, intersecting with a three-section, 30-foot elevated main display. Adorning the display were three large ice carvings, the largest of which was carved to resemble a spectacular Waterford Crystal vase, which was filled with three dozen red roses interspersed with green leather ferns. The vase alone weighed more than 200 pounds and took four people on ladders to hoist it to its elevated position, creating a beautiful centerpiece that could be seen from any seat in the room.

The display also featured three large white wicker baskets filled with colossal strawberries from Driscoll, a leading berry supplier. The strawberries had been hand-dipped in two kinds of chocolate with white chocolate tips, and mixed with baby's breath, to resemble floral arrangements. Also on hand were fresh-fruit carvings, fresh vegetable displays, a mega-shrimp cocktail at the base of a carved-ice dolphin, and numerous salad and other cold offerings.

Food stations, manned with cooks, stood ready to prepare omelets to order, shrimp scampi, sliced steamship rounds of beef, carved roast turkeys and baked Tavern Hams, waffles, and roll-your-own tacos. Four six-foot long serpentine tables graced the entrance of the Club Room arranged with over three dozen desserts to choose from. We put the desserts front and center to artfully encourage guests to save room for them and dine more selectively on the Grand Buffet's other selections.

On the Saturday before Mother's Day, after finishing the dinner business, I moved on to last-minute food preparation for the next day's buffet. Some of the cook staff had also stayed over after their Saturday shifts, and they headed home at 2 a.m. Jim stopped by around 3 a.m., setting off the burglar alarm and scaring the shit out of me. It's spooky being by yourself in that large a building in the early morning hours. Jim was surprised to find me still working.

"I love you, man!" he shouted. It was obvious he appreciated my work ethic and my willingness to do whatever it took to get the job done. From my point of view, there wasn't much of a choice. Jim unlocked the bar cabinet where the Louis XIII Cognac by Rémy Martin was stored. He came back to the kitchen with the bottle and snifter glasses and poured two shots.

"Here's to a great day tomorrow," he toasted. Down the hatch they went. Then Jim said, "Let's have another." On the second, I took my time, slowly sniffing then sipping the expensive spirit, which had a retail cost of more than $100 a shot. The stuff lit me up like a Christmas tree and warmed me all the way to my toes.

"Tomorrow's going to be a home run," announced Jim, leaving as quickly as he'd arrived. As it turned out, the Cognac was just the stimulant I needed to keep me going. Revived, I was soon back in the thick of it, moving ahead with a precious second wind.

I worked all through the night—the crew started to straggle in at 6 a.m. We were up against a 10 a.m. deadline that was fast closing in. The crew had been pushed hard all week, but even starting at 6 a.m. the staff was left with a daunting amount of work still to do. Everyone knew there was no time for chatting or smoking, and we all chased our tasks at a feverish clip. At 10 a.m. on the button, with the parking lot already half full and guests lined up at the front door, the Grand Buffet was ready to be served. We had over 900 reservations and more still coming in.

Mother's Day, more than any other day except Easter, is about family. Everyone dresses to the nines; children run about wide-eyed and excited, moving through the dining rooms, while the wait staff hopes mom or dad will keep them from disturbing other guests. This Mother's Day, the atmosphere was electric. Our maitre d' and wait staff looked impressive in their black-and-white tuxedo-style uniforms. The cooks wore spotless white chef coats and black-and-white chef pants. I even donned my large pleated toque.

The steady flow of guests meandering into the Club Room turned into a torrent within the first hour. All the local movers and shakers were present. Omelets were being flipped, roasts sliced, shrimps sautéed, waffles browned and tacos stuffed to overflowing. The shrimp cocktail display, always a favorite with buffet goers, was taking an early hit. The dessert tables, initially unmolested, began to diminish as the first wave of guests marched up to them from their seats.

Walking through the room, I was in my glory. Happy and smiling, I enjoyed explaining the various food preparations to the foodies in the crowd and receiving their accolades. But my main concern was the food supply. It's the chef's responsibility to calculate the popularity of the foods that will be consumed and make sure the restaurant has enough stock. I could see from the start that today's volume had been more like an educated guess and would require constant attention. From the look of the plates passing by me, the pyramidal piles they supported, and the large number of guests, maintaining today's supplies would prove to be a challenge.

It's standard practice to have back-up supplies ready to go as hungry eaters deplete the initial displays, and we had back-ups aplenty for everything today. But just four hours into service, the shrimp cocktail began running low, exhausting even our back-ups. We broke out another case of shrimp and hurriedly began steaming, peeling, and deveining them and sending them out to the cocktail display, while holding back several pounds of raw shrimp for sautéeing at the Scampi Station.

The scramble was on and—with our attendance off the charts—I feared a trip to the dreaded weeds might begin any minute. Jim popped his head through the swinging kitchen doors to excitedly tell us we had just passed 1,500 served! Our advertising strategy had worked, if anything, too well. With most of the cooks manning buffet stations, only one other cook, myself, and two busboys were left to replenish the buffet. My goal was to keep ourselves just above the weeds without slipping into C.F. territory. But the calls kept coming, calls for more bain-maries of whipped eggs for the omelets, more waffle batter, more meat and fixings for the tacos, still more shrimp, and for back-up supplies of roast beef, turkey and baked ham. Many of the salad offerings also needed to be pulled from service and refreshed.

Stamina is one of the most important traits a chef can possess. Over the years, you learn to function on sheer adrenalin and work through any number of aches and pains. I had racked up over 30 consecutive hours with no end in sight. The effects of the Louis XIII Cognac were long gone, along with my second, third, and fourth winds.

Meanwhile, everything was running out at the same time. The team in the kitchen hardly knew what to do next. Our activities had morphed into a full-blown cluster fuck. As commanding general of operation Grand Buffet, I headed to the front lines on a recon mission. I rendezvoused with the maitre d' in the lobby, and was blown away by all the people still waiting for tables.

"What the hell's going on?" I asked the maitre d'.

Just then, Jim joined us. "Len, everyone's raving about the food, the great atmosphere and what a good time they're having," he said, beaming with delight. "You're the man. Great job! How about another drink?"

"Make it a double, I need it!" I'm often asked why chefs drink. Do I have to explain any further?

The maitre d' informed me there were almost 400 more reservations to go over the next four hours. OMG. All I wanted was to lie down, shut my eyes, and enjoy a nice foot rub. Heading back to the kitchen, I stopped by the buffet stations and instructed them to cut back the portion sizes as we had a long way to go.

The dessert display, by now, had been reduced to a mess. Cheesecake chunks, chocolate curls, berry drippings, and broken cookie pieces lay scattered about the white table coverings. The diners had found their stride and made short work of our hard work creating the display. In the kitchen, with most back-up stocks gone, we were preparing food to order. I was shouting orders at my sparse crew—running on instinct and adrenalin.

"Get another four cases of desserts out of the cooler," I demanded. "Plate them up as needed and clean up the dessert table. Get someone to drain the pans under the ice carvings. They're about to overflow onto the buffet trays. Bring out another case of shrimp and thaw it under running water. Crack and whip up another case of eggs. Season three more Tavern Hams and get them in the oven. Cut up more produce and wash another two flats of strawberries. Make more waffle batter and refresh all the taco station condiments."

I would have used a swagger stick except I needed both hands free to help. We pushed on, grinding through the remaining hours of service. By early evening, with just 15 reservations left to serve, the C.F. had extracted its toll. The entire staff was drop-dead exhausted. I finally sat down in the swivel chair in my office and finished a watered down drink. Once in the chair, I found myself unable to rise. Midge, my wife, helped by a dishwasher, wheeled me out to the car and dumped me into the passenger seat.

The Grand Buffet was over. It was little short of a miracle we'd pulled it off. The final tally was over 1,900 men, women, children, and a couple of seeing-eye dogs served. I later heard the day's receipts were north of $40,000. After a 36-hour shift I desperately needed, and deserved, a rest. Yet, even as I headed home, the dishwashers were still totally snowed with full trays of dishes, sacks of garbage, and an untold number of empty boxes lined up outside the building in the employee parking area. On my return, at 7 a.m. the next day, the dishwashers were still finishing the dishwashing so we could begin again with the new day's business.

DINING OUT

Dining quite exquisite at improved Jaussaud's

By PETE TITTL
Californian staff writer

The buzz of a winner wafts through the air at Jaussaud's. The Union Avenue landmark, which reopened under new management last spring, has a new dinner menu, but this is not a desperate act aimed at pulling in customers. They're already there. Go early on a weekend night and the place is two-thirds full, and the customers look happy. It's an older crowd, and I suspect they are comforted by the revival of a place they probably frequented while younger. Jaussaud's, like them, is a survivor. Only now it's thriving.

In my 1992 year in review restaurant column last week, I named Jaussaud's as one of the two most improved restaurants in town. Although the physical refurbishing was done in 1987, it took the new crew, led by executive chef Leonard Gentieu, to restore the kitchen's glory. It's a pleasure to see a place with history being resurrected so assuredly.

The dinner menu, introduced about two ...

REVIEW

JAUSSAUD'S
1001 S. Union Ave.

Phone: 321-9810. Reservations recommended.

Hours: Lunch 11 a.m.-2 p.m. Monday-Friday. Dinner 6-11 p.m. Monday through Saturday. Sunday brunch 10 a.m.-2 p.m.

Prices: Appetizers $6-$9.50, dinners

Caution

A few more cautions: Bacardi 151 Rum is very flammable, so keep the bottle away from the open flame, and only flambé a small amount at a time. On occasion, some burning rum may end up on the outside of the glass or on your hand. Don't panic. If on the glass, it will burn itself out; if on your hand, pat it out with your other hand. Several seconds have to elapse before you receive a severe burn. Finally, keep a small fire extinguisher hidden away, just in case.

FIRE WALK WITH ME—FLAMING COFFEE À LA GENTIEU

Flaming Coffee a la Gentieu, as I like to call it, is a dessert you can drink—a rich, delicious brew that raises table service to performance art because it really is a show when done properly. I've performed this coffee service for hundreds of people and taught it to scores more in my cooking classes. One student, a rabbi, served it to 32 people at a synagogue function. He said they loved it.

The preparation involves live flames and great care has to be taken not to light yourself or anything close to you. As I recounted in a previous chapter, I did this early in my career in front of a roomful of V.I.P. guests, before whom I became the flambé, escaping with my hand slightly burned and my ego charred to a crisp, so I speak with some authority.

I cannot emphasize enough the care and practice this dish requires unlike, say, Serrano's Chile Verde (recipe on page 132). Practice it on your own before attempting to serve at the conclusion of a dinner party. Several video clips on You Tube, under the heading "Flaming Coffee," demonstrate proper technique. Watch them.

My son Greg introduced Midge and myself to this coffee when he was working at the Red Lion Restaurant and Hotel in Bakersfield, California. He suggested I offer it to the smaller parties I serve through my catering business and to students in my cooking classes. He also mentioned it was guaranteed to yield a good tip.

Flaming Coffee à la Gentieu

To begin, you will need glassware that can withstand the heat of burning rum. I use a 17.5-ounce Lilly 8418 Bolla Grande wine glass that has worked well for me over the years. You will also need:

Ingredients:

Brewed coffee
Kahlúa
Baileys Irish Cream
Bacardi 151 Rum
Ground cinnamon
1 Fresh orange
Sugar
Fresh whipped cream

You will also need a flame, preferably from a candle. Start by quartering the orange and using one piece to rim the edge of each glass with its juice. Dip each orange-rimmed glass into sugar placed on a small plate as if you were rimming a margarita glass with salt. Next, pour a scant ounce of rum into a one-ounce ladle. I prefer Bacardi 151 Rum, a highly flammable variety that's 75.5 percent alcohol.

Holding the ladle in one hand and the glass in the other, run the ladle over the open flame to ignite it. Place the burning ladle of rum halfway into the glass. Carefully lift and tilt the ladle upward and out of the glass, catching the burning rum in the glass. When the ladle empties, blow out any remaining fire in the ladle. Swirl the glass with the burning rum as if it were a red wine. Sprinkle some ground cinnamon into the fire to create a colorful sparkling effect.

The rum should burn for several seconds, but don't let it burn too long as the glass will become too hot. Pour the coffee into the glass by resting the edge of the coffee pot or container on the edge of the glass. When you begin pouring, move the glass in a downward motion and the coffee container in an upward motion. This causes a stream of coffee to flow through the air to half fill the glass and extinguish the flame.

Add shots of Kahlúa and Baileys, a dollop of fresh whipped cream, and sprinkle with cinnamon. When handing the drink to the guests, caution them about how hot it is. This dish exists in many versions using a broad range of ingredients. Once you're comfortable making it, experiment with coffee syrups, other liqueurs and chocolate.

This coffee service is even more spectacular performed in the dark. The rum burns with a beautiful blue flame and sprinkled cinnamon adds a "Fourth of July" effect. Just be sure there's enough light to let you see what you're doing!

CHAPTER 22

THE DAY FROM HELL:
Free Wine and That Sucks

"I hope we didn't ruin it by taking so long with the shrimp. I owe you an apology for that," I said. "Normally we're nowhere near that slow."

Not a problem, well worth the wait, everybody agreed. The prawn platter was delicious—every bit as good as Jean said it would be.

"That makes me feel better because it's been one of those days," I said. "Unbelievable! We're short-handed, two parties were booked just this morning, we had a flood in the kitchen and all of this happened on one of the busiest days we've had all year."

Art picked up on that. The parking lot was so full he had to circle it five times before finding a space, he laughed, and the travails I just recounted to the group explained all the frenzied activity he saw when he stepped inside. Why it had the look and feel of, well a CF, he chuckled.

Did I hear what I thought I heard? Indeed I did, as Art confirmed with a knowing wink. I was tempted to respond that not only was he right, ours was the worst kind of CF—an FBCF, but in deference to the sensibilities of the other guests, our conversation shifted to a milder form of disarray—being "in the weeds."

"Hell, I've been there and felt the pain," Art said. "My first year at college I worked in a steak house, a big one, and there were some Saturday nights I just wanted to walk off the floor. I don't know how you do it, day in and day out."

"I often wonder that myself. How long did you work there?" I asked. We were fast becoming buds.

"I only lasted a year, but the experience taught me a lot. I developed a work ethic that's stood me in good stead ever since. What I learned in that steak house you can't be taught in college, and after that experience I've always been patient with service when I eat out. I know your cooks went the extra mile today for our lunch. Here's a little something for them."

DAY FROM HELL

And with that, he placed half a waffle—a $50 bill—in my palm, and even though it had been me who knocked out the shrimp, I passed it on to the cooks.

With the lunch rush behind us, we began setting up the line for dinner, the cooks' morale lifted by Art's generous tip. I was beat, and still had the dinner shift ahead of me. The joys of ownership—the owner keeps going while the day shift goes home.

By mid-afternoon, the night shift began arriving. "Margie, get together with Sam," I said, "and fill him in on what needs to be prepped." Sam was the lead night cook. It's always a good idea for the two shift leaders to talk about what has to be done for the dinner service. It brings the night cooks up to speed, and lets them know what backups to prepare to avoid a trip to the weeds.

"Len, Alan's here to take tomorrow's food order," one of the servers informed me.

"Send him in."

Alan was the salesman for the supplier who shorted the chicken breasts on our morning delivery. Putting that aside, he was a good salesman, and usually earned the bulk of our food purchases.

"Hey, Alan, what the hell happened to the chicken breasts?" I griped when he came in the kitchen. "The shortage really put me in a bind!"

"Man, Len, I'm sorry. Someone in the L.A. warehouse screwed up and had them in the wrong slot, causing a back order code to kick in. By the time I got the message on the shortage, the truck had left the ranch. The slotting issue's been resolved and I can have the breasts delivered with tomorrow's order."

"Well, that's reassuring, considering we served the party we needed those breasts for three hours ago. Do me a favor. At your next sales meeting in L.A. be sure to let the warehouse manager know what a fine job we think he's doing and to keep up the good work. It's good to know we can count on him as an important link in our supply chain and know he'll have us covered with critical supplies during crunch times."

Just a little sarcasm for Alan to let management know it had an unhappy camper, "right here in River City." He picked up on the jab right away, and changed the subject, but I'd made my point.

"Len, we better get the order taken," he said. "We have less than an hour before the cut-off for delivery tomorrow."

"Okay, I'll have the manager grab the order guide. Oh hell, she's out sick today." Allegedly. "Almost forgot. I'll have to handle this. Let's start with the frozen food."

"You got it."

No sooner had I finished giving Alan the order than the cashier peeked through the kitchen door to tell me my 4 p. m. appointment had arrived. "Tell them I'll be right out," I said. What appointment is that?

I ran to the office and threw open my day timer, and there it was—Mrs. Stewart and her daughter Mary Lou wanted to meet to discuss catering

Mary Lou's wedding. Having to contend with one disaster after another, I hadn't had the time to check my appointment schedule. O' endless day! My appearance was disheveled and I was hardly in the mood to meet with these two gals, but…

"Hi, Mrs. Stewart. And this must be Mary Lou."

"Mary Lou, meet Mr. Gentieu. He's the chef and owner of the restaurant."

"My pleasure," I said, and asked if either of them would like a glass of wine as we headed to the Gaslight Room to discuss Mary Lou's catering needs.

"That would be nice, we both like rosie." Rosie?

"I'll have one of the waitresses bring it to you."

"Won't you be having a glass?"

"I wish I could," I answered, "but I still have to work the dinner hour and need to prepare the menu items." What I needed was a tall whiskey and Coke, and after this meeting I meant to have one—dinner hour or not.

Wine served, our discussion began. After gathering the basic information about the date, time, and number of guests, and explaining how our guarantee works, I tried to nail down a budget number, the number that determines the food and wine options that are available as we custom-design the menu to meet the customer's preferences.

At times it can be awkward, even embarrassing, if the number is too low. A couple once came in with a budget of $15 per person, hoping for a chicken dish and a nice white wine to go with it. I almost didn't have the heart to tell them that budget would cover little more than an assortment of nuts, potato chips and dip, with Coca Cola as the beverage. That was a party we did not book.

"Do you have a budget number in mind?" I asked Mrs. Stewart.

"Well, the kids are just starting out and want to save money for their honeymoon cruise," she answered. "Say, could we have another glass of that rosie? It's tasty!"

Not looking good, I thought. I didn't know these people from Adam, and already they were gulping down my wine and looking for prices low enough to subsidize the newlyweds' honeymoon cruise.

"We have a friend who works at a brewery and can get the beer wholesale," Mrs. Stewart went on, "and family members who can make the salads, so you won't have to." This was going nowhere, and I needed to get ready for the dinner rush.

"You know, ladies," I told them, "I think we might not be the right venue for Mary Lou's wedding from what you're telling me. Our insurance and liquor licenses do not allow food or beverages to be supplied from outside sources."

Mary Lou's response was short and to the point: "That sucks."

Oh so true my dear, but there was nothing I could do about all the restrictions and government regulations we had to adhere to. My hands were tied, I said, and we were unable to deviate from the rules.

**DAY
FROM
HELL**

"The government has its hand in everything!" Mrs. Stewart groused.

"You are so right," I sighed. "It makes it hard for small businesses like ours to compete. Ladies, I'm so sorry we cannot do your wedding."

"Do you know another place, reasonably priced?" Mary Lou asked. She was beginning to get a little bit of a buzz on from our fine rosie.

I suggested giving the YMCA a call.

"We checked with them already, and just to reserve the reception room will cost $800, and that's without food. That won't leave us nearly enough to pay for the honeymoon cruise."

"I have to excuse myself and get back to the kitchen to cut the steaks for the dinner hour. I'm sorry I can't help you."

"Thank you so much for the wine!"

After politely escorting the Stewarts to the door, I stopped by the cashier's stand. "Len, you look a little pale," Linda, the cashier said. "Are you feeling all right?"

"Been a rough day, and those two were a piece of work, but don't worry about me—just have someone bring me a 20-ounce Coke, half full. I'll be in the kitchen."

I kept my private stock of whiskey in the kitchen—but none of the cooks were allowed to drink on duty but me. Rank, after all, does have its privileges. When the Coke arrived, I placed it on the cutting board that served as my private bar, and watched the whiskey gurgle into the soda cup. Then down the hatch. The whiskey and Coke disappeared after three or four big gulps.

A drink now and then helped me cope with being a perfectionist about the presentation and quality of every dish we prepared, so much so that the crew actually liked seeing a 20-ouncer sitting on the cutting board. Call it a weakness or a crutch, whatever you will, I didn't feel guilty about having an occasional drink on duty.

I placed several freshly butchered steaks in the cold drawer near the broiler. The steaks had a bright red bloom from having just been cut, and would be fit for a gourmet after coming off the broiler. From Sam, the lead night cook and Margie's evening counterpart, I learned that the *mise en place* was in good shape for the dinner hour.

"What about the French fries and breaded shrimp? Do we have plenty prepared?" I asked Sam, with the lunch shortage still fresh in my mind. He assured me that we did, and all was ready for the dinner rush.

CHAPTER 23

In the Country of Clubs, Part II

After Jaussauds fell victim to the lousy economy and closed, I created a catering business, and secured a management contract to operate the Bakersfield Petroleum Club, which led me to accept the House Manager's position at the Bakersfield Country Club. My second experience in the Country of Clubs.

As House Manager, I was responsible for overseeing the food and beverage service, banquets, catering, the snack bar operation, special-event barbecues and food service for the many golf tournaments the club hosted. Everything to do with dining and house operations fell under my leadership.

I came on board soon after the Club had undergone a complete tear down and rebuild at a cost of several million dollars. The Club was one of the finest in Kern County with the best golf course in the area. I was excited and ready. I was also, I thought, uniquely qualified, having by then had years of restaurant ownership experience, a strong kitchen background, C.I.A. schooling, and nearly two years of cooking for generals.

One of the biggest adjustments I had to make as House Manager was adhering to the Club's dress code. I was expected to wear a suit and tie every day except casual Fridays. Suits and ties were a radical change from my normal attire of checked chef's pants and the white double-breasted chef's coat I'd always worn in Leonard's.

Christy, the Club comptroller, served as my personal fashion cop. Every morning, she looked me over and gave me either a thumbs up or recommended a change. One day, I missed the mark so badly she suggested I return home and start over. Luckily, Christy's husband, Jim, was a real clothes horse. Jim took me under his wing—on a shopping trip to the outlet mall, I quickly spent $4,000 suiting up under his direction. He did such a nice job that my wife, Midge, started showing a renewed interest.

I would also be dealing with Club politics. Christy, a veteran employee, had seen managers come and go and had a acquired a broad knowledge about the Club's issues and personalities. She was very bright, had many friends on the board, and knew the pecking order, especially who was in and who was out. She understood what was really important amid all the Club chatter, a talent I found invaluable. Realizing I needed her on my team was immediately apparent, but I also wanted her as a friend. We ended up having a great, mutually respectful relationship and made significant improvements during my tenure, especially regarding Club finances.

It was made clear to me when I was hired that the board was concerned about how the Club was hemorrhaging money—more was going out than coming in. They wanted a manager to make the tough decisions needed to bring costs under control, a task well-suited to my restaurant and back of the house experience.

The previous manager and staff had, I learned, spent what they wanted. The idea that it was acceptable to run deficits was hardly unique to the Bakersfield Country Club. It was, in fact, as prevalent as a bad flu among private clubs. After all, ran the logic, the members had lots of money and would always make up short falls through end-of-year allocations. This is what had been going on before I arrived.

In reviewing the books, it became clear that many of the operation's critical percentages were seriously out of whack. Unless procedures were changed quickly, the year-end monetary penalty to the members would be so great the Club restaurant's hours of operation would have to be greatly curtailed.

I met with Christy to devise a six-month plan to turn things around. The centerpiece was to better use the facility's catering capability to increase sales. Brent, our Catering Coordinator, was instructed to go after all the parties he could book. Catering was more profitable than day-to-day dining and would provide the revenue needed to help bring our percentages back in line.

Volume cures a multitude of sins, but increasing revenue was only part of the equation. Controlling costs and eliminating waste were equally important. Great care has to be taken when making cuts at a private club to preserve the quality and service standards at the levels members expect. This made cuts the most difficult area, by far, to work through. But we sharpened our knives and quickly put them to use. With Christy's support, I was soon laying off staff and adjusting schedules, menu prices, and Club services. We also examined food and beverage suppliers, many of the Club's sacred cows, which had been quietly subsidized over the years. Everything was on the table, including my popularity rating, which I was sure would be taking a hit along the road to fiscal health.

Did I mention excess spending? And internal politics? There was more of both than I care to relate, but one item in particular tested my managerial mettle. The Club employed a personal trainer who worked in the men's fitness room. A handful of members used his services a couple days a week, but the trainer's hourly rate did not even come close to supporting the limited service he provided. He was a nice fellow, but his services amounted to a hidden subsidy for the few members he trained. I informed him we had to eliminate his position, and suggested he would be allowed to charge the members individually for his services and still use the Club fitness room.

The news that the Club trainer was gone quickly reached the workout folks. One member, a doctor, stormed into my office asking who the hell I thought I was to let the trainer go. He demanded a meeting in an effort to reinstate him. And, indeed, a meeting was held. About 20 other Clubbers joined the doctor in his cause. Still furious, the doctor soon had the group fired up and looking for a little piece of me, though only a few actually used the fitness room, much less the trainer's services.

As the rancor intensified, I imagined myself Daniel in the lion's den. I listened intently as the doctor itemized all the reasons the trainer was needed, and how the club had provided his services for years. There was no lack of insults hurled my way, along with many suggestions that I had better watch my step, as I was new on the job.

Then it was my turn. I asked how happy the members were about the increasing allocations of the last several years. I mentioned that the board of directors, which they elected, had ordered me to get costs under control. I told them about the solution the trainer and I had discussed, which I thought would work for everyone and be in the Club's best interest. The whole issue died at the next board meeting, with the board supporting my action. I don't believe any member of the group that confronted me ever personally retained the trainer.

Brent, meanwhile, was booking large wedding receptions, birthday parties, anniversaries, and corporate meetings. The food and beverage department was generating thousands of dollars in sales with party invoices ranging from $10,000 to more than $20,000. To allay the Club's initial nervousness, I signed for many parties booked outside the Club membership, personally guaranteeing the Club would be paid.

Within the first year, the food and beverage department was showing a profit in excess of $20,000 per month for several months running. We had turned a negative number positive as our operating percentages vastly improved. Most board members were businessmen who understood the significance of the rapid turnaround. They diverted most of our profit to grounds and golf course maintenance, but that didn't matter to me. We had created a profit center.

At the year-end, state-of-the-Club board meeting, I presented a report about our progress. Using charts and graphs that took me weeks to create, I showed the board what had been accomplished. The board loved it. Everything was great.

But I remembered something a previous Club manager told me. He had spent his whole career in country clubs and predicted I would earn one or two enemies at the conclusion of my first year, five or six by the end of my second year, and two or three more in each of the following cycles. By year five or six, I would have enough enemies within the Club that they would be able to get rid of me.

I wasn't sure how many I already had, other than the doctor, but my longing to live along California's Central Coast had been growing stronger. After two and a half years, I decided not to stick around and test the prediction—I would pursue my dream of living by the ocean and owning a yacht. I was proud to have worked at the Club, and learned a lot about management. Christy and many members remain friends to this day.

But I had grown restless.

Serving Suggestions

Serve with flour tortillas and Spanish Rice. Good versions are made by Goya, Zatarain's, Rice-A-Roni and Knorr Fiesta Sides. Add more Jalapeño to make the chili spicier.

EASY AS UNO, DOS, TRES— SERRANO'S CHILI VERDE

I first tasted Serrano's Chili Verde over 20 years ago at the Bakersfield Country Club, where I was the General Manager. It was one of the club's main dishes and often served as a lunch special. Fidencio Serrano, the first cook at the club, learned the recipe, an authentic Mexican version, from his mother. We all looked forward to it. How simple it is to prepare is the most surprising thing about the recipe. Whenever he made it, the other cooks tossed tortillas on the open fire to heat, then spooned in helpings of the Chile, rolling up the tortillas for quick, flavorful snacks. It happened every time a pot showed up on the stove.

Serrano's Chili Verde

Ingredients:

2 lbs. pork butt, cubed
1 large yellow onion, diced
10 cloves garlic, minced
20 tomatillos, outer skins removed
3 large Jalapeño chili peppers, roasted and diced
5 Tbs. cumin, ground
2 cans green enchilada sauce
1/3 cup lard
Flour tortillas
Chicken stock, optional
Salt and pepper to taste

Start by melting the lard in a heavy roast pan or skillet. Add the onion, garlic and pork, browning over medium heat. Brown the tomatillos in a hot oven. When the pork browns, add the tomatillos, Jalapeños, cumin and enough enchilada sauce to cover the meat, then stir. If necessary, add enough chicken stock to fully cover the meat. Season with salt and pepper, and slow cook covered in the oven until the meat is tender.

CHAPTER 24

THE DAY FROM HELL FINALLY ENDS

I put the day's events behind me and got myself in the mindset needed to tackle the upcoming dinner hour. Having the *mise en place* was essential, but having a shift run smoothly meant coordinating a lot of moving parts and personalities. And if I survived the dinner hour I would still have the half-hour drive home before mercifully ending this nightmarish day.

Thinking about the drive home reminded me of the splatter on my windshield from the morning bombardment, and I asked Johnny, the night shift dishwasher, if he would help me out and take care of it.

"What the hell hit your windshield?" he asked me after finishing the job and returning. "I had to use a spatula to get that shit off."

"Yeah, whatever it was must have been big."

"Could have been an ostrich jumping up on the hood while you were waiting for the light," Johnny opined. "They can leave a load that big." During the day Johnny worked at an ostrich farm—yes, they exist in California—and one of the ostriches kicked the bejeesus out of him once. They were constantly on his mind after that.

Just as I settled in on the cook line I was summoned to the cashier's stand, where a middle-aged man was arguing with our night manager. The guy was wearing a short sleeve shirt with a floral design, checked Bermuda shorts, a baseball cap, and a light blue fanny pack under his pot belly—not exactly the look of a winner.

"Hi, I'm Leonard, the owner," I said, extending my hand. The guy wouldn't shake hands, and that pissed me off from the get go. He had a mad on, and had me lined up in his cross hairs. I suggested that we step into the banquet room to discuss what was upsetting him, since it's never a good idea to expose other guests to a potential altercation.

"How can I help you Mr.—?"

After identifying himself he alleged that one of our customers put a dent in his car door while he was shopping in Bernie Goldman's clothing store.

DAY FROM HELL

134

"How do you know it was a restaurant customer?" I asked, already suspicious of his story. Bernie didn't stock fanny packs, or any of the rest of the apparel this guy was wearing.

"Had to be one of your customers. The car that hit me was parked in front of your place." The lines for our parking spaces were allegedly too narrow, which caused the incident, he said. He didn't want to submit a claim to his insurance company, and demanded that I pay for repairing the damage to his car.

I had encountered this kind of complaint before—someone assumes that because I own a restaurant the "deep pockets" concept will apply and I'll roll over, open my check book and foot the bill. He said he knew the town planner, and could cite the code I was allegedly in violation of.

I'm sure he thought this thinly veiled threat would intimidate me, but I wasn't buying it. Having already been through an FBCF, I was ready for this jerk, and in no mood to be hustled for the cost of fixing a car without even knowing whether the damage actually occurred in our lot.

I grabbed the phone book and quickly paged through it. "Let me help you in your quest for justice," I told this asshole. "Here's the town planner's number. If you want to research the code with him go right ahead. Right now I need you to leave the restaurant. My dinner hour's ready to start and I've wasted too much time with you already."

We have to be on our toes dealing with situations like this. There are folks out there who are always looking for something to sue you for. As a restaurant owner or manager, you have to be eternally vigilant in everything relating to the operation of the business. That means having your guard up when someone like the jerk who tried to rip me off comes through the door.

The dinner hour having begun, I returned to my place on the cook line. With a fresh wheel man calling, ordering, firing and pick-up, I was back at the broiler station, which was getting the most action. Tired or not, I switched gears from drive to overdrive. The other stations on the line were not as busy, so the cooks were able to help out on plate-up.

I was the best broiler man in the house, and the right person to be on that station. It's important to set up the broiler with the temperature zones adjusted for the cooking times of the different menu items. The hottest section is used to quickly sear steaks before moving them to a cooler spot to slowly reach their desired levels of doneness. Exceptions are orders for Pittsburgh style and à la Chicago steaks. A Pittsburgh-style steak is also known as a "black and blue" because it's charred black on the outside, but rare and bloody (blue) on the inside, while steak à la Chicago is first cooked to the right doneness, then quickly charred.

At Leonard's, we broiled steaks to less than the desired doneness, then finished them over a hot Oakwood fire at the last possible minute before service. Some customers will request that a steak be prepared "mooing," or just "walked over the coals," meaning the steak is rare to the point of being cool at its center. That's too rare for me, and I think "black and blue" is less flavorful than a nice brown medium rare, but it's the customer who's paying, and it's our job to prepare the steak to his or her liking.

A skilled broiler man or woman is a great asset. His or her skill and experience is the key to a smoothly running cook line. At any given moment an assortment of steaks, chops, fish, burgers, lobsters, even vegetables may be broiling away. Most chefs are able to handle it all from memory, having heard an order only once, when called out by the wheel man. Keeping it all straight, and sending the right item out when it's ordered, as it was ordered, time after time, is second nature to them.

The dinner rush was in full swing, and I was loving every minute of it. As chef and broiler man, I set the attitude and the pace. The broiler was covered with food and we were concentrating hard and working fast, playing the symphony conducted by the wheel man. Some were jumping in to assist, while others stayed at their stations waiting for orders, but the whole team was tight and totally committed.

The restaurant was packed with people waiting to be seated, and the night manager checked in on us to make sure everything was okay. The back-up stock was holding fine. Keeping the orders moving out of the kitchen was the only thing we had to worry about.

"The people at Table 6 said they were the best New York steaks they'd ever eaten, cooked to perfection," exulted Jaimie, a waitress. "We love it when you're working the broiler," she added before going back to the dining room, "the orders come up fast and the customers are happy." Smart girl. I liked her.

The dinner rush was generating an entirely different vibe than the lunch hour had. This was the way things were supposed to be. The restaurant needed to make money, not only to meet the staff's payroll, but to spin off a profit for the owner. Today that would happen—business was good.

Then, in a flashback to this morning's disaster, Johnny hit me with the news that the pot and pan sink was not draining as fast as it should be and the dishwasher's rinse and drain cycles were running too slow.

"I don't believe it! Check the restrooms right away and see if there's any trouble there." What the hell was wrong with the sewer system now? Jesus, the blockage had been cleared just this morning!

"Len, no problem in the restrooms," Johnny reported when he returned. "Whatever it is, it's limited to the kitchen." Limited. That at least was a break.

"Get Susie back here, quick!" I instructed Johnny. Susie was our night manager.

"Len, what's up?" she asked.

"You and Johnny see if you can find what's causing the problem with the kitchen drains. If you can't, give B-B-Ben a call and tell him we need him again."

Fifteen minutes later, Susie reported that she and Johnny had had no luck finding what the problem was, and had called Ben, who arrived ten minutes after the call.

135

"Ben, thanks for getting here so quickly," I said when he came in the kitchen. "We've got another emergency, two in one day if you can believe it."

"W-w-where's the trouble?"

"We know it can't be the main line, so let's see if we get lucky again and try the other clean-out outside."

Without so much as a shake of his head and no lip sucking, Ben agreed, and went back to his truck to fetch the electric snake and the sheet music for "Hit the Road Jack." After Johnny ran the extension cord outside and equipped Ben with a pickle bucket, he was in business again.

Meanwhile, orders for menu items that had to be broiled had backed up, warranting another whiskey-flavored Coke. After a quick belt I was back on the broiler pulling off steaks for pick-up when all of a sudden I heard something rattling around underneath the rubber mat I was standing on. When I looked down, I saw a sight straight out of a Stephen King novel.

Ben's snake had somehow escaped, and with its curved razor-sharp blade of a tongue, had chewed its way through the mat and was now headed for my feet. "Johnny!" I shouted as loud as I could, "tell Ben to turn this goddamned thing off!"

By now the snake was about a foot above the floor and writhing like some wild sea creature in a horror movie. I didn't dare try to grab it for fear of getting my hand sliced open, and danced a little two-step to avoid the whirling blade while I chucked steaks off the broiler. Thankfully Ben turned the power off before the thing could rear up like a cobra, poised to strike a vulnerable part of my anatomy.

I stared down at the business end of the now flaccid coil of stainless steel and counted my toes while the cooks on the line laughed hysterically.

Somehow or other, possibly because he had his nose in the Ray Charles chart, Ben had managed to miss the clean-out with the snake, and after a "m-m-my bad, m-m-my bad," tried again, and eventually cleared the drain. Another remnant from the dish towel had caused the blockage.

With all the drains now running freely, Johnny was able to catch up on the unwashed service ware that had accumulated during this latest crisis. The rest of the dinner service was uneventful; soon the orders slowed to a trickle.

The nightmarish day was drawing to a close. The other cooks could finish the remaining orders and take care of cleaning the cook line. I headed to my office to put my feet up on the desk and refuel with one last cup of coffee before heading home. The night manager would "z-out" the registers, meaning tabulate and print out the day's transactions, balance the cash drawers, post the sales, and after locking up, drop off the day's receipts in the night deposit box at the bank across the street.

Before driving home I looked up at the night sky. It was clear and illuminated by a bright full moon. I reached over to the radio to turn it on, but changed my mind and sat back to reflect on the day's events. A day that had begun with love in my heart had been an unmitigated disaster. I looked up at the sky again. Do geese fly at night? Or condors? I started the engine. The windshield should be safe from attack, I thought as I pulled out of the parking lot.

Arriving home, I greeted Midge with a hello and a kiss on the cheek, and asked if the kids were asleep.

"Yes, thankfully," she answered. "They went to bed about an hour ago after wearing themselves out fighting all afternoon."

"Hey, I've got an idea. Why don't we head to the bedroom for a little love making?" That, at least, wouldn't be interrupted by a plugged dishwasher.

"Honey I'm tired. Why don't we just cuddle? It's been a rough day. How was yours?"

"Oh, same old, same old. Cuddling sounds good."

"Where's your shorts?" Midge asked me as I undressed.

"It's a long story. I'll tell you about it after I take a nice hot shower."

"That might not be a good idea."

"Why's that?"

"After the kids showered I started the laundry, and there wasn't any hot water. Something must be wrong with the water heater, but before I called the plumber I thought I'd wait till you got home and checked it out."

"Are you kidding me?"

"Look on the bright side. At least the kids got clean. You can take a corina. You don't need hot water for that."

A "corina" is cook's slang for a sponge bath—a quick wash of the face, armpits and groin with a damp towel. Often on Friday nights, after closing, cooks would hurriedly clean the line, take a corina, splash on a little aftershave and head out to party.

"What the hell, it figures." I said.

After my corina, I joined Midge in bed. She turned off the nightstand light, snuggled close to me, and whispered, "Sorry about the hot water."

"Ah, honey, don't worry," I told her. "Things could be worse." Boy, could they ever!

She reached over and kissed me. "I love you."

"Hey," I said, and pulled her close. "I'm good with that."

Epilogue

Hands gripped my shoulders, shaking me. Faintly, I heard Midge telling me to wake up. What the hell was going on? I didn't want to move, didn't want to leave my dream.

Midge's voice grew urgent, "Len, Len, get up," she said. "The charter group's here and the Captain's ready to cast off. Wake up Len—wake up!" Startled, I turned over, half awake, and faced her as she repeated the words that had shattered my sleep, "Wake up, wake up. We need to get under way."

I sat up and blinked. Reality flooded back with the warm sunlight on my face. It was 2006, a beautiful spring day, and I'd been catnapping on the foredeck of the "Papagallo II," our 72-foot yacht.

I'd been reflecting on my career, thinking that today's chefs were outpacing me. What had I done lately to keep up with these guys? Had I grown complacent? In my heart I was still a competitor, but something was missing. The old Len was missing, the Len who started and managed restaurants. That was when I was always happiest, when I felt I was accomplishing something worthwhile—or so I'd thought as I nodded off, after prepping the food for an afternoon charter.

"Honey, are you alright?" interrupted Midge. "You look confused."

"I do?"

"Were you having a bad dream?"

"I don't think it was a dream."

"Then what?"

"Not sure. It was like something from the twilight zone. 'Write the Book', I remember someone saying."

"Write a book? You're a chef, not a writer."

The Captain interrupted us to say we needed to begin the charter. "Sorry, Cap, I'll grab the stern lines," I said.

The lines were quickly cast off. Captain Randy Ryan sounded three short blasts on the horn and we gently slipped from the dock.

The ship's bar opened and the charter guests stepped up for the first of many rounds. The yacht's speed increased as we glided through Morro

Bay Harbor, where we are based. The ship's Detroit diesels were giving us a comfortable speed of about 10 knots, but we could feel more than hear the thrum of the engines. We were headed toward the open sea on a clear, bright afternoon.

The sea was turquoise blue with slight swells, and a gentle wind blew from the northwest. A pod of dolphins crisscrossed our bow as we went out the harbor's mouth. Captain Ryan brought us up to cruising speed, which seemed to make them even more playful. The guests leaned over the rails as the dolphins' dorsal fins cut through the water—sleek agile bodies racing back and forth in our bow wake, just below the surface of the water, within inches of the boat.

Captain Ryan set a north by northwest course to take us offshore about six miles. Randy Ryan is an excellent captain and a well-respected mariner. He has a master's license, knows our harbor like no one else, and has worked everything from tugs in San Francisco Bay to the 200-foot "October Rose," when it was owned by Kirk Kerkorian. I always have to convince Ryan to wear his Captain's uniform, which he affectionately called "the monkey suit," but our guests love taking pictures with him in uniform.

"Thar she blows!" hollered the first mate, playing it up for the onboard audience as if he was a mate in Moby Dick. "Captain, whales off the port side."

Captain Ryan quickly changed course to head for them. "Barkeep!" called a guest "Another round for a toast to the whales." And the drinks were duly poured.

Captain Ryan was careful not to maneuver too close, not wanting to disturb the massive animals. The guests were in awe of their majestic beauty and the steady rhythm of their diving and blowing. Leaving the whales to their migratory journey, Captain Ryan resumed his course, and everyone settled in to enjoy food, drinks, and conversation.

"So if it wasn't a dream, what happened to you?" Midge asked me on the foredeck. "From the look on your face when I woke you, I thought something must be wrong."

"This is going to be hard for me to explain," I began.

"The experience was more like a vision or a premonition. The setting was fantastic, out of this world. I was in a gigantic banquet hall, more opulent than anything I've ever seen. A stage was centered in the room with an ornate carved podium. Hundreds of people sat at beautifully appointed tables throughout the vast space. The tables were elegantly set with fresh flowers and crisp white linens. The service was gold, the glassware was fine crystal and candle-bearing centerpieces burned brightly."

"Honey, you haven't been chewing weed, have you? How can you recall all this in such detail?" Midge asked.

"A Who's-Who of the food industry was in attendance," I continued, "including chefs I've never met, just read about or seen on TV. There were even chefs from centuries past dressed in period attire. Real masters like Auguste Escoffier—the king of cooks and the cook of kings— Pierre de Lune and Prosper Montagne. I felt honored to just be there."

Midge leaned in as I described how an orchestra in black tuxedos, led by a conductor dressed in white, supplied the classical background music.

"The food was extraordinary, too," I went on, "with buffets presenting a cornucopia of the world's cuisines. Fruit carvings ranged from watermelon baskets filled with edible flowers to an underwater coral reef made of fruit. Cold plates displayed seafood, game birds, wild boar and venison. Ice carvings rested in a dry-ice fog on lighted multi-colored platforms packed with dry ice."

141

The lights dimmed as if a program was about to begin, and everyone took their seats. My table was in front of the stage, just left of the podium. With a drum roll, an elderly man, who looked to be 100, came onstage and made his way to the podium. The gentleman had a full head of wavy snow white hair and wore a black pinstripe suit and black shoes shined up to military standards.

I realized, with a shock, he was the old waiter I worked with at the DuPont Country Club early in my career—the person who gave me the single, key word of advice ("percentages"). The old gentleman tapped the microphone.

"Friends and colleagues, I want to extend a warm welcome to all of you," he began. "Tonight we conclude this year's Epicurean Rendezvous with a very special award."

The old waiter now had the audience's complete attention. "It's no secret epicureans strive to live luxuriously through the enjoyment of gourmet food and fine wine," he said. "That's what attending the E.R. is all about. And epicureans are by no means conventional in our zest for life. We are often haughty, egotistical and ego driven."

"Often, in our quest for the finer things in life, we become detached from the function of daily living. We lose our vital connection with the genuine people around us. In the culinary world, these are the people who carry out the day-to-day tasks required to feed and serve everyone. They play remarkable roles on the grand stage of life and overcome many obstacles to do their jobs. They are the unsung heroes of the restaurant business. Tonight, we epicureans would like to recognize their success by honoring all those for their hard work and service with the Thanks for Being There Award."

"Right now," I told Midge, shaking my head in amazement, "Sharing all of this with you—remembering what he said in such detail—has made me wonder what the dream meant, and why I dreamed it."

Midge and I were called away again just then—a couple was celebrating their anniversary and we joined in the toast. But while pouring bubbly and watching people chatter and laugh over cake and champagne, my mind raced.

The old man's closing words from my dream echoed. The words, "We epicureans would like to recognize their success," had really hit home for me. Over the fifty-plus years of my career, I've worked with thousands of people. After all these years in the food-service trade, I am reminded how important an asset these people are to the success of the establishments that employ them.

The people working within a company are that company's most important asset. This holds even more so for the service sector—businesses like restaurants. Yet, wait staff, busboys, line cooks and dishwashers garner very little recognition for the hard work they do.

Many of these positions are entry-level jobs—work hours are usually long and the pay meager. But without these people, restaurants would not be able to operate. These positions make the ordering, service, and preparation of the food, along with the clearing of the tables and washing of the service ware possible; they are at the very heart of every restaurant.

Too many customers, and even some employees perceive the work the rank-and-file perform to be menial. The person performing these essential tasks is "just a waitress," or "just a busboy," or "just" a cook or dishwasher. The perception is a negative one, placing these staff members low on the social scale just because their positions don't fit the general perception of what success is.

There was a chill in the air as the cruise was nearing its end. The guests returned to the salon to warm up. Midge and I remained on the foredeck. It was the magical few minutes just before sunset. Across the horizon the sky deepened to tangerine tinged with shades of purple and red. The setting was breathtaking, the sky's color tranquil; the sea calm, its surface ablaze in gold. The roll of the yacht was light and soothing.

Standing there, we began laughing as we recounted how the adventure of owning the "Papagallo" began. Thinking how stunned Graham, the yacht broker, was when he asked what size boat I was moving up from—a sailboat or cabin cruiser? I replied that up until that point all I'd owned was a 12-foot kayak that I paddled around San Simeon Cove, just below Hearst Castle. Graham asked if I realized what was involved with yacht ownership—the pitfalls, expenses and the commitment it would take to own a 72 foot yacht. At the time, I was hell bent to make my boyhood dream a reality and assured him that somehow I could make a go of it. Midge was in Graham's camp, not at all "on board" with the idea of creating the yacht charter and dinner-cruise business we were about to embark on. (Thankfully, she came around during the sea trials before escrow closed, at which time we became the new proud owners of the "Papagallo II." While motoring under the Golden Gate Bridge, Midge looked around and said, "I could get used to this.")

Just as we looked up from our conversation, we witnessed the green flash as the sun dipped below the horizon. Despite all my time at sea, this was the first time I had ever seen one. Ancient Egyptians believed those fortunate enough to witness it would find their lives changing for the better from that moment on. Day had softly turned to evening. Night at sea did not so much fall as rise, the sky turning dark blue then almost black as the sunlight faded.

In the wheel house, Captain Ryan fired up the engines and set our course for port two hours away. Arriving at the dock, the passengers, along with the crew, disembarked and headed home.

Midge and I decided to spend the night in the yacht's master suite. In the morning there would be the usual post-cruise cleanup. I set the timer on the coffee maker and we retired below to sleep. Waking early, we went topside to watch the sunrise while we had our coffee.

All around us in the harbor gulls squawked as they searched for food, pelicans dive-bombed sardines and harbor seals barked on the floating dock. Sea otters were cracking open and eating crabs they had caught on the bay's bottom. This was a typical morning in our yacht-based office and I realized, yet again, how blessed I was to live and work in such a beautiful place.

Any thought of being outpaced by younger chefs and not being able to keep up in my career, or growing complacent, had vanished from my mind. Enjoying our ninth year, Papagallo Yacht Charters is a success. We're living our dream in this new venture—vastly different from owning and operating our previous restaurants. A dream that began when I was 10 years old was now a reality, forty-five years later.

Coffee in hand, I headed to the yacht's office, grabbing my yellow legal pad and began to write. Cleaning up the yacht could wait. I needed to get my thoughts down on paper.

Midge came by my desk, peered over my shoulder and read aloud the words I had just jotted down: "I did not grow up in the family restaurant business, but…"

"You're already writing the book," she said, and smiled.

Afterword

Knowing how challenging the restaurant business is, I feel compelled to reach out to the work force.

If you are a service industry worker, don't get caught in the trap of letting others determine your self worth by attaching a "just" label on you. Do not give up on yourself. Change your attitude from "I can't" to "I can."

It's easy to feel discouraged and unappreciated for any number of reasons: "My family life is a mess." "I have a drinking problem." "I have a drug problem," or even, "I don't have the skills to advance above my current job." Too often that's used as a reason for doing only what is necessary to get through each shift.

Choice is available to everyone, and one's place in life has everything to do with the choices he or she makes. Use your current situation as a stepping stone for improvement. It's not easy to initiate change—I will be the first to admit that—but change is what it takes.

Begin with a leap of faith, keeping in mind that the journey is everything. There is nothing mediocre in nature, nor in you when you choose not to accept mediocrity. You can pick up the paint brush and begin painting the image you desire on the canvas of your life. Why? Because no one else will.

There's always a payoff for doing your best. Hard work and dedication will be noticed by owners, managers, co-workers and customers alike. And your willingness to go the extra mile, your ability to get along with customers and co-workers alike and your compassion towards others will be repaid. That payment may not be at your current job—it can take place when you least expect it, sometimes months or years later in life. But it will happen. It's a natural law. Expect it.

Dreaming and visualizing what can be will open the door to possibilities. One crucial move is to take action, to act. If you desire advancement, start now without worrying about what others may think. Don't allow them to hold you back.

I encourage you to think hard about your goal. Make it big enough and think about what it could bring your way. Dream it, visualize it, talk about it; go for it and embrace it. Without a strong goal there is little reason to act.

The principles I'm sharing with you are based on eternal truths. My purpose in reaching out is to bring these principles to your attention and encourage you to reset the targets in your life and aim higher.

As a service employee your contribution is critical to the success of your establishment. Your numbers collectively far exceed those of the celebrity chefs and TV personalities across the nation. Simply put, you make restaurants work! Take pride in the services you provide, starting right now.

Accept the symbolic award presented by the old waiter at the Epicurean Rendezvous. Accept our gratitude. You deserve it.

The writing of this book is only the first step for me, a foundation to build from. I'm not at all sure where it will lead. I envision an interactive web space that anyone, not just food service workers, can visit—a site that's open 24/7, where people can share experiences, ideas, successes, challenges, encouragement and much more with their peers. It will be a safety zone where people can go to take that first step toward a better life; a site where food service people and others can connect with each other, share dreams and build incredible, fulfilling lives.

I am still on the journey, but with less of an idea now of where the final destination will be. That doesn't really matter, because this is just the beginning.

PHOTO BY JESSE ACOSTA

Cuis

BY KATHY MARCKS HARDESTY

How to live large

Sit down and set
sail for a delicious
dinner party

ON DECK
Chef Leonard
Gentieu works
from a tiny gal-
ley to prepare
sumptuous
meals for diners
as they cruise
Morro Bay.

*Maison
De
Gentieu*

*TROIS
FEUILLES
AU VENT*

**2013
PASO ROBLES
CABERNET SAUVIGNON**